CHRIST AND CONSCIENCE

CHRIST
AND
CONSCIENCE

N. H. G. ROBINSON

B.D., D.LITT.

Professor of Systematic Theology in the University of St. Andrews

JAMES NISBET & CO. LTD.

22 BERNERS STREET, LONDON W.1

First Published 1956

Printed and bound by
Butler & Tanner Ltd., Frome

To
MARY ELIZABETH
I affectionately dedicate this book.

CONTENTS

PREFACE ix

PART ONE
CHRIST AND CONSCIENCE

I. THE CLAIM OF CHRIST 3
II. CHRISTIAN FAITH AND MORAL RESPONSIBILITY . 21
III. THE CHRISTIAN INTERPRETATION OF MORALITY . 55

PART TWO
CHRISTIAN THEOLOGY AND CONSCIENCE

IV. BARTHIANISM AND EVANGELICAL THEOLOGY . . 85
V. TOWARDS A MORE ETHICAL EVANGELICAL
THEOLOGY 104
VI. CROSSROADS IN THEOLOGY 123

PART THREE
THEOLOGY AND THE MODERN MIND

VII. THEOLOGY AND FAITH 147
VIII. THE BIBLICAL SITUATION 171
IX. MORALITY AND MYSTERY 193

INDEX 219

PREFACE

THE purpose of this work is not to outline a system of theology. It is to perform a preliminary but indispensable task, for its aim is to identify, define and defend a theological perspective, one from which the truth and errors of liberalism, as well as the strength and weaknesses of such a movement as Barthianism, can be seen. This theological standpoint is that of ethico-evangelical theology. Accordingly, it is argued that the claim of Christ, though not merely moral, is yet moral through and through ; that certain ethical objections to Christian faith cannot be finally sustained ; and that, on the contrary, Christian faith has its own account, positive and negative, of our natural moral condition, of mere morality and of the full reality of the moral life. It is further maintained that Barthianism, while it is an evangelical theology, is to be more precisely characterised within that field as a type of evangelical theology which is non-ethical, metaphysical and radically empirical ; that amongst those who have come closest to Barthianism there is discernible a movement towards a more ethical evangelical theology ; and that, as a matter of fact, evangelical theology as a whole reveals a quite distinct alternative to Barthianism. In a final section, the particular perspective on which the discussion turns is brought into relation to some of the principal trends, both of theology and of philosophy, in the modern world.

In following out this argument I have made some use of material already published elsewhere, and for a ready and kind permission to do so I am greatly indebted to the Editors of *The Expository Times* ("Dr. Niebuhr's Religious and Political Thought," April, 1951, and "The Importance of P. T. Forsyth," December, 1952), of *The Hibbert Journal* ("Karl Barth's Empiricism,"

July, 1951), and of *The Philosophical Quarterly* (" Natural
Law, Morality and the Divine Will," January, 1953).
Such material, however, I have freely adapted to its
place in the present argument.

N. H. G. ROBINSON

PART ONE
CHRIST AND CONSCIENCE

PART ONE

CHRIST AND CONSCIENCE

CHAPTER I

THE CLAIM OF CHRIST

A T the centre of the Christian faith and the Christian religion there is not, as has often been supposed, a doctrine or a proposition but a personal encounter, not a belief *about* someone or something but a meeting *with* someone. This has always been the case throughout the history of Christianity. It is as true of apostolic times and of medieval times as of any other age. Wherever there has been a living and genuinely Christian faith there has been this personal encounter at its root and centre. It was this that transformed the outlook of St. Paul as he took his journey towards the city of Damascus, and it was this that justified him in declaring, " I live ; yet not I, but Christ liveth in me." It was this too that determined the form of St. Augustine's *Confessions*, written, it will be remembered, in the first person and addressed to God in the second, for this form of prayer and confession is in the hands of St. Augustine not simply an artifice of literary invention but a form of religious expression more fundamental and more original even than theological argument. Behind the elaborate and intricate system also of St. Thomas Aquinas' thought and theology there lay " the mystical life " of the saint, no less real and no less central even though, as M. Maritain has said, there is " never a direct statement by himself, for he practised only too thoroughly the maxim of St. Anthony the hermit which he may have read in Cassian . . . that ' there can be no perfect prayer, if the religious perceives himself to be praying.' " [1]   And it is to this element of personal encounter that Martin Luther turned in his essay on *Christian Liberty* when he wished to point to that which

[1] Jacques Maritain, *St. Thomas Aquinas* (Sheed and Ward), p. 47.

3

makes a man a Christian. "The soul has no other thing either in heaven or upon earth whereby it can live, and be religious, free, and Christian, except the holy Gospel, the word of God preached by Christ " [1] in which God "sets you face to face with His beloved son, Jesus Christ." [2]

Further evidence of the existence of this personal relationship at the very heart of religion is to be found impressively in the fact that there has always been on man's side a desire to withdraw and escape from it when its reality has been most forcibly brought home to him. At such a time Simon Peter could exclaim, "Depart from me ; for I am a sinful man, O Lord " ; and the Old Testament tradition has its own instances as notable as those of the New. "Oh Lord, thou hast searched me and known me," cried the psalmist, "thou knowest my downsitting and mine uprising ; thou understandest my thought afar off. . . . Whither shall I go from thy spirit ? or whither shall I flee from thy presence ? " "I have heard of thee by the hearing of the ear," said Job, "but now mine eye seeth thee. Wherefore I abhor myself, and repent in dust and ashes." And Isaiah's prayer was not essentially different, "Woe is me ! for I am undone ; because I am a man of unclean lips, and I dwell in the midst of a people of unclean lips ; for mine eyes have seen the King, the Lord of hosts."

So far then from this personal relationship and encounter with God being a figment of the human imagination or an addendum to the religious reality made by the human mind when it came to reflect upon it, it is itself a reality from which in some of the highest reaches of religion the human spirit has been anxious to escape. This, let it be repeated, has always been the case ; but it has not always been theologically recognised. The personal relationship has always been there, but the intellectual apparatus with which theology has been equipped for the execution of its task has not always

[1] *Op. cit.*, para. 5   [2] *Ibid.*, para. 6.

been sufficient to insure the adequate representation of this relationship and, especially, of the fact that it is a relationship. On the contrary, there have been long periods when the picture presented by theology has been such that one might well have supposed that the centre of the Christian faith and the Christian religion was after all occupied, not by a personal relationship at all, but by a doctrine, by a proposition the subject of which, even the author of which, was held to be God, and to which the Christian in virtue of his being a Christian offered his assent. There have been long periods when, in other words, theological work has been marked by a rationalist bias, a rationalist cast of thought, which was derived from the prevailing intellectual apparatus of the day and which determined the form in which theological truth was inevitably expressed. Indeed it is only in the modern period that this bias has been partially over-come—partially, I say, for of course there are still in contemporary speech and even in contemporary thought many traces of it, as when we talk of Christians as believers, for the distinction between " believing in " and " believing that " does not really deny or disguise the predominantly rationalist origin of the very idea of believing in this connection. It is only in the modern period that the rationalist cast of thought has been partially transcended and superseded and a more ade-quate intellectual apparatus evolved. Indeed it may well prove to be the fundamental mark of the modern period in theology that at last the personal relationship involved in all living Christian faith has been theologically recognised. It is after this that Schleiermacher, Kierke-gaard and Ritschl were all striving in their different ways, and it is almost impossible now to revert to a thoroughly rationalist system of thought in theology without a con-scious and deliberate return to the Middle Ages.[1]

---

[1] Thus a Roman Catholic writer like D. J. B. Hawkins offers his treat-ment of his theme quite " frankly as a natural theology on the medieval model." *The Essentials of Theism* (Sheed and Ward), p. 14.

Broadly speaking, the difference between the mental approach, the intellectual apparatus, of the modern period and that of the ages of rationalism is that where-as the latter is predominantly speculative the former is almost exclusively interpretative. For the rationalist outlook the function of reason was to transcend what was given, and on the whole the given itself was largely despised ; while the modern age may well be thought to have begun whenever this transcending power of reason was called in question. From that time the true function of reason has been increasingly regarded as that of enlarging, organising and interpreting the given ; and in the modern period the work both of philosophy and of theology may be very largely understood as the search for an ever more adequate empiricism. The rise and growth of empirical science is one of the most outstand-ing products of the modern spirit and has often been noted as the characteristic achievement of the post-medieval age.[1]   But it is not the only typical attainment to reflect the change in mental approach. The picture of the human situation as essentially a social situation in which we find ourselves face to face with other self-conscious beings and in which we communicate one with another is also symptomatic of the change. It is a curious fact that Plato, who made such brilliant use of the form of dialogue in his philosophical work, was yet prevented by the rationalism of his age from seeing its implications for philosophy itself, and that although his philosophical arguments and conclusions are pre-sented in the course of one conversation after another they themselves do not portray anything like a realm of ends or a society of minds, but only the activities of a universal, almost impersonal, reason. It is equally curious that, in spite of the form of St. Augustine's *Confessions*, the early Christian era and the Middle Ages

---

[1] *Cf.* John Macmurray, *The Boundaries of Science* (Faber, 1939), p. 9, where he says that " the creation of science is . . . the peculiar contribu-tion of Western civilization to the development of human life."

remained as rationalistic as those which had gone before, and were blind to the implications for theology of the supreme revelation—the Word made flesh—by which living souls were confronted by the living God ; and also that that revelation should have been theologically assimilated to the traditional products of reason, receiving its classical expression in the medieval synthesis and appearing therein as a supplementary proposition to those which a transcending reason could reach by itself. There were of course important differences between the pre-Christian outlook and that of the medieval world. Professor Paul Tillich has argued in one of his earlier papers that while Greek philosophy was " a struggle against fate, an attempt to rise above fate ",[1] the victory of Christianity meant " the radical denial of the demonic character of existence as such " [2] and that " what was created was not Hellenism, but *Christian Humanism.*" [3] Such a change can scarcely be overestimated, but it should not be allowed to obscure what remained very much the same in both periods. Fear of fate and faith in the Fatherhood of God are two radically different phenomena, and yet it was with very much the same intellectual apparatus that the ancient and medieval worlds respectively sought to deal with the philosophical and theological problems which they raised ; and it was not until the modern period that this mental approach underwent a radical transformation, although of course the beginning of the change and the preparation for it can be traced at a much earlier date.

This latter change itself is an important one which it would be foolish indeed to underestimate ; but even so it is to be remembered that it is a change in the mental approach, in the intellectual apparatus, with which the modern mind attacks the problems both of philosophy and of theology. In particular, in the latter sphere it has to be borne in mind that Christian faith has always

---

[1] Paul Tillich, *The Protestant Era* (Nisbet, 1951), p. 5.
[2] *Ibid.*, p. 8.   [3] *Ibid.*, p. 9.

involved a personal relationship with God and that it
is only the theological recognition of this relationship
which has been delayed until comparatively recent times.
Yet there is a tendency in certain strains of contemporary theology to regard theological rationalism as by
its very nature, not just theologically, but also spiritually, immature, indeed as involving a flight, an attempt
to escape from the presence of God, an endeavour to
immobilise God by regarding Him as an object to be
thought about and not as One whose thoughts are
greater than ours and who confronts us in judgment
and in grace.   Such strictures on theological rationalism, however, are most naïve, and those who make
them seem to forget that God is not only greater than
our faith but greater still than all our theological formu-
lations of that faith.   It is simply not true that throughout the ages of rationalism God allowed Himself to be
reduced to the inert subject of a theological proposition.
No doubt there were individuals then who allowed their
rational theology to come between their souls and the
living God and to provide a substitute for religious
faith, just as there may be individuals today who allow
the Barthian theology or any other to do the same ;
but that fact should not be a tenet of any theology but
a warning to all, and its recognition is certainly the
monopoly of none.   Indeed these strictures on rationalism betoken a twofold blindness, a blindness, first,
to the intellectual limitations within which, inevitably,
earlier ages had to work, and a blindness, in the second
place, to the debt in which all modern theology stands,
whether it recognises it or not, to a transformed mental
approach and an intellectual apparatus with which other
ages were not endowed.
   It is with these considerations in mind that the point
is made that whereas Christian faith has always involved at its very centre a personal relationship with
God and has been a living with God and not simply
a believing in Him, this fact has not always been theo-

logically recognised, and that indeed its theological recognition is the outstanding, peculiar and characteristic merit of modern theology. This in itself is no mean advance, but it is a theological advance and not one which implies or confers any spiritual superiority. It betokens a greater reflective insight into the mystery of Christian faith, perhaps into the mystery of God Himself and of His dealings with His children, but it does not in the least guarantee a more humble and wholehearted obedience to God's claim upon human life. Similarly, in the moral sphere there are many simple-minded people who cannot begin to define the nature of a moral obligation but who are, none the less, quick to recognise and answer one, quicker, it may be, than many who understand the general situation better.

Moreover, it is only to be expected that, although the recognition and representation of the personal relationship present in all living faith are the great achievement of modern theology, all modern theology does not display them in the same degree. There is even a type of theology which harks back deliberately to the medieval rationalism which the present age seems destined to supplant ; and there is another type which seems to have a foot in both camps, since it re-affirms the general position of rationalism but allows a larger scope to the empirical tradition in the provision of adequate grounds for a theistic rationalist argument. Furthermore, even when the very method and principle of rationalism are condemned and firmly set to one side, and when the recognition of a personal relationship is allowed to come into its own, there are varying degrees of adequacy with which it is represented as a *personal relationship*. This in fact is the crucial question which confronts the most influential theological school of the present time, that of Barthianism, for it may well be doubted whether, in its way of regarding the personal relationship between God and man which it is so concerned to stress, this theology does conceive of it in a manner adequate to its personal character. And this doubt is only expressed in other words when it is questioned, as it may well be questioned, whether the Barthian theology is an ethical theology.

Certainly it is a thoroughly evangelical theology, and it is to the credit of Dr. Barth that he has given to the modern age a vigorous and impressive re-statement of the Protestant evangelical faith, and that he has done this at a time when its peculiar insights were in danger of being blurred and even lost under the sway of theological liberalism. If, as W. P. Paterson maintained, it is the mark of liberalism to emphasise what it calls the general " revelation " to reason and conscience, and if on the other hand it is the supreme function of evangelical thought to concentrate attention upon the specific revelation of God in the Person of Jesus Christ His Son, and, especially, upon the atonement as, in P. T. Forsyth's phrase, " the one key to His person," [1] it is easy to see that Dr. Barth's radically Protestant theology must be classed as an evangelical theology and as one wholly opposed to liberalism. According to Dr. Barth the so-called " revelation " to reason and conscience is not a revelation at all, and it provides neither a preparation nor a point of contact for the revelation in Christ. Even Dr. Brunner's admission of the bare uncorrupted forms of reason and conscience, whatever they may be, as a point of contact is dismissed by Dr. Barth as in germ a return to liberalism, and it is evident that, for the latter, liberalism is not just a seriously inadequate version of the Christian faith which urgently requires to be supplemented and thereby transformed, but is rather a rival to be destroyed root and branch. From this point of view revelation must be understood as *in every way* creating its own response. This is a highly paradoxical position, and it does seem plain that it leaves no room at all for a personal relationship, for

[1] P. T. Forsyth, *The Cruciality of the Cross* (Independent Press, 1948), p. 4.

a relationship that is personal in something more than
name. In his later work it is not clear whether Dr.
Barth wishes openly to withdraw from this earlier standpoint and unsay some of the things that he said with
considerable vigour in his celebrated controversy with
Dr. Brunner ; but at any rate he does see some need
to acknowledge the place of reason in the constitution
of faith, which is the response to revelation. " Christian
faith," he says,[1] " is not irrational, not anti-rational,
not supra-rational, but rational in the proper sense."
" Christendom and the theological world were always
ill-advised in thinking it their duty for some reason or
other, either of enthusiasm or of theological conception,
to betake themselves to the camp of an opposition to
reason." [2] Thus reason is involved in faith, but it is
reason completely determined by its object which, in
turn, is not an object at all but altogether subject,
namely, God. It is reason wholly determined from outside itself. But if this qualification is taken seriously, as
it is obviously meant to be, can it be reason which is
thus wholly determined ? Is it not the name only that
has been given back and not in any sense the reality ?
Is reason still reason when it is wholly immobilised
and made, one must suppose, like molten wax ? And
whether it be still reason or not, does not this complete
loss of its native powers spell the end of any possibility
of a personal relationship ?

None the less there is truth in Dr. Barth's contention.
In faith I *am* wholly determined by God, by His revelation of Himself in Jesus Christ, not to the immobilisation
of my rational and moral powers, but rather to their
illumination and increase. In faith I am *both* wholly
determined by God *and* wholly self-determined as well.
This would indeed be a great coincidence were it not
that God " has made us for Himself alone and our
hearts are restless till they rest in Him." " Faith is

[1] Karl Barth, *Dogmatics in Outline* (S.C.M. Press, 1949), p. 23.
[2] *Ibid.*, p. 22.

really self-disposal," said P. T. Forsyth,[1] but it is self-disposal in relation to a God who claims us wholly, completely, for Himself. Dr. Barth emphasises almost exclusively the latter half of this truth, and he has even something to say in defence of doing so.

> By the silence of the Confession on the subjective side, by its speaking only of the objective Creed, it also speaks at its best, deepest and completest about what happens to us men, about what we may be, do, and experience. . . . Whoso means to rescue and preserve the subjective element shall lose it ; but whoso gives it up for the sake of the objective, shall save it. . . . This " I believe " is consummated in a meeting with One who is not man, but God, the Father, Son, and Holy Spirit, and by my believing I see myself completely filled and determined by this object of my faith. And what interests me is not myself with my faith, but He in whom I believe.[2]

There is manifestly truth in all this and important truth, but it lies on the practical level of living faith and not on the reflective level on which we stand back and examine this faith (subjective and objective) which is ours. These two activities, the life of faith and the vocation of theology, must not be confused, or else we come near to saying by implication that it is only the theologian who can be saved, whereas in fact, as we have seen, he stands in daily peril of allowing his theology to become a barrier to salvation, and he does so whatever character his theology may have. Faith itself must certainly look outwards to God, not inwards to man ; but theology cannot escape the responsibility of considering the response to revelation as well as revelation itself, and although it may not be able to say much about it in a positive way it may be able to avert misunderstanding and unnecessary offence. Christian theology has no power to extract the native scandal from the Gospel, but likewise it has no right to make them " sad whom God hath not made sad."

There is, however, another element in Dr. Barth's

[1] *The Cruciality of the Cross*, p. 71.   [2] *Dogmatics in Outline*, p. 16.

antagonism to the idea of a theology of the subjective as well as the objective, and it is to be found in his conviction that " we never believe ' on account of ', never ' because of ' ; we awake to faith in spite of everything." [1] Here too there is truth, but the intransigently universal form in which it is expressed is only possible in a rigidly one-sided theology. In faith our whole existence is judged but it is also fulfilled. We believe, because of certain things which point in that direction, in spite of others which do not, but, above all, because God commendeth His love towards us in that while we were yet sinners Christ died for us. This is not just one positive consideration amongst others, both positive and negative ; it does not lie on the same level as these ; it is the all-sufficient reason which embraces and gathers up everything that would lead us towards faith, and which deals adequately with everything that would hold us back.

There is, moreover, in Dr. Barth's mind still another reason for his exclusive attention to the objective side of faith. Just as, rightly, he will not allow that we believe because of this, that and the other particular reason, so, in like manner, he would doubtless refuse to admit that we believe in Christ rather than in X, Y or Z, rival objects for our faith. This is the truth contained in his persistent denial that " we men bear in us a capacity to meet God, to hear His Word," that is, a capacity for faith. The truth is that some believe in God and some do not believe at all, not that on the level of faith they put something else in God's place. Idolatry is not false faith but essential sin. When, wholly determined by God and yet wholly self-determined as well, we have faith in God, we do not choose God rather than something else as the object of our faith. God chooses us and no-one else could choose us in this way. Either we have faith in God or we do not have faith at all. Does not this mean, however, that

[1] *Ibid.*, p. 20.

the determination is all from without, that there is no
self-determination and no freedom in this matter ? The
presupposition behind this suggestion is of course that
freedom and responsibility and self-determination all
imply choice and that choice implies a plurality of
objects ; and yet if this line of thought does lie behind
Dr. Barth's indifference to subjective faith, it is a line
of thought which is shared by those who criticise an
evangelical theology on the ground that we are not
responsible for a sin to which there is no alternative,
and, moreover, it is a line of thought which is quite
mistaken. We *are* responsible, entirely responsible, for
that in which wholeheartedly we acquiesce, whether
in faith or in sin, and irrespective of the presence
or absence of any alternative course of action. In
particular, in the present connection, we are fully responsible when in faith we apprehend Christ and are
apprehended by Him, and this in spite of the fact that
we do not, as it were, choose a suitable object for our
faith, this object or that. In this sense Dr. Barth is
quite right in holding that we have no general capacity
for faith, a capacity, that is to say, which we might
exercise in this direction or in that.

Might it not be said, however, that although we do
not choose between objects of faith, we do choose, in
the moment of decision, between having faith, that is,
faith in God, and not having faith at all ? Yet when
this suggestion is taken seriously it reveals at once its
inadequacy. How could we possibly choose between
faith and no faith ? " To whom shall we go ? thou hast
the words of eternal life." There is no choice here, but
there is an entirely responsible decision and self-disposal.
The choice proposed between faith and no faith is an
unreal choice—like that between having one's breakfast
and emigrating to America. The alternatives suggested,
faith and its absence, are imponderables and incom-
parables ; we cannot choose between having faith and
not having it. There are indeed choices connected with

faith which lead up to it, choices which prepare the way for it or perhaps postpone its advent as they did in the case of St. Augustine ; and there are choices which stem from it, choices between following the course which the faith we have dictates and travelling some other easier road. But faith is not involved in the choices which lead up to it ; and it is already presupposed by those which stem from it—they are choices, good or bad, of a Christian man, a man who has faith. But when faith itself is born we are born. It is an activity of the whole man in response to a divine claim which lays hold upon the whole man. There is here neither a meticulous weighing up of reasons for and against nor a deliberate choice between rival contestants. Faith is no less than self-disposal in relation to One who claims us utterly for Himself. It is on the objective side wholly determined by God who reveals Himself from without, but it is wholly determined at the same time, on the subjective side, from within, wholly self-determined. It is true to say, as in fact P. T. Forsyth has already said,[1] " we believe because he makes us believe—with a moral compulsion."

" I believe—of course ! " says Dr. Barth.[2] " It is my, it is a human, experience and action, that is, a human form of existence. But . . ." But can there be any " buts " here ? Is not this a very part of the miracle of grace that it is I who am claimed and that it is I who believe ? " Lord, I believe, help thou mine unbelief." To relegate all this in theology to a mere parenthesis is to run the serious risk of an arbitrary one-sidedness. It is not only to run counter to all our pastoral practice and belief but it is also to reduce the mighty movement of God's grace to something no more dramatic and no more personal than the progress of a steamroller. On the other hand, if faith is, as it certainly seems to be, both wholly determined by God and

[1] P. T. Forsyth, *The Justification of God* (Independent Press, 1948), p. 47.
[2] *Dogmatics in Outline*, p. 16.

wholly self-determined, it involves what is fully and completely a personal relationship, *the* personal relationship in which all others are re-shaped and re-born. The creative impact, then, of the revelation in Christ is not a blind, mechanical impact ; it constitutes rather a claim upon a man's whole being and existence, that is to say, a moral claim.

No sooner, however, is that said than it requires to be elaborated in two different directions at the same time, for it needs to be added that this claim of Christ is a *moral claim*, and, secondly, that it is not simply *a* moral claim alongside other and similar moral claims.

It is, however, a *moral claim*, for confronted by it we are treated as persons and indeed are treated fully and entirely as persons for perhaps the first time in our lives. For we are treated not just as the imperfect persons that we are but as, in the making, the perfected persons we may become. " I have called thee by thy name, thou art mine." When Abraham prayed for the cities of Sodom and Gomorrah he laid an intolerable weight upon the five righteous persons who might be found within their precincts ; but Christ when He comes sees in the eternal salvation of one " lost sheep ", whether it be this man or that, an adequate justification of the whole creation, of its indefinite preservation, and of His own saving mission therein. " When thou shalt make his soul an offering for sin, He shall see of the travail of his soul and be satisfied." This means that, beyond all doubt, we are treated as persons, as ends, indeed as the end and justification of everything else. And yet it is curious that a theology which sees so clearly the personal character of God's self-revelation, which sees so clearly that the revelation is to be found in the Son whom God sends, the Word made flesh, is slow to allow the highly personal nature of His activity. It seems even more curious when it is realised that to be thus slow is virtually to dismiss as the small dust of the balance the world of difference which lies between a personal activity and a physical or mechanical force. Certainly Barthian theologians do allow that there is freedom in the Christian life, that the Christian life makes men free, but they tend simply to place this freedom alongside the complete determination from without which they are even more concerned to stress. This can hardly be regarded as a satisfactory procedure, even when the conjunction of determination and freedom is described as a paradox beyond our powers to understand ; still less satisfactory is it when one side of the paradox is stated only parenthetically as " a secondary matter . . . small and unimportant." [1]

Moreover, even when it is stated, there is often a serious ambiguity, for it is never quite clear whether the Barthian theology asserts that in faith, in the very act of faith, I am free or that I am made free by faith, that my freedom presupposes faith. Even when Dr. Barth tells us that " that which I do in believing is the only thing left to me, to which I have been invited, to which I have been *made* free by Him who can do what I can neither begin nor accomplish of myself ",[2] the ambiguity remains. This is not a matter of splitting hairs. Rather on this issue it depends whether a theology is to savour of morals or of mechanics, whether revelation is to be represented as the miracle of grace it is or as a miracle of sheer omnipotence. Nor does it seem very doubtful in which direction the truth really lies. In faith I am not just passive, passively receptive, wholly inactive. On the contrary I am spiritually alive as I have never been before. I am wholly determined from without in the sense that God fills my horizon ; but I am also wholly self-determined for all that I am acknowledges Him to be my Lord. I am made free to come to Him precisely by His coming to me in mercy, in Christ ; but clearly it is a material freedom that is here conferred, the matter and content

---

[1] *Dogmatics in Outline*, p. 15 ; but *cf.* Luke vii, 9, and xviii, 8.

[2] *Dogmatics in Outline*, p. 18 (italics mine).

of my formal freedom which is mine, which is myself. And when the revelation comes home to me it is not a kind of spiritual operation that I undergo, it is a claim that I have to meet, a claim which comprehends my whole being, past, present and future, and shuts out everything else, a claim with no competitors, a claim whose impact lifts me to a higher level of existence, but still a claim. Of course, in a sense, there is more than a claim here, and it is this fact which causes confusion. Besides a claim, there is a judgment, a judgment upon my whole existence, and there is also a gift, the gift of a new existence. A claim, then, a judgment and a gift—but they must not be separated and treated as essentially successive phases of the soul's experience. Thereby we reach the concept of a scheme of salvation, a human scheme of divine salvation, which is a moral and religious self-contradiction. Judgment and grace are distinguishable but inseparable aspects of this claim, Christ's claim upon our lives ; and confronted by Him, we know nothing of a judgment which is not permeated through and through by divine grace, nor are we aware of any grace which does not claim us completely for itself. " The Spirit and the bride say, Come. And let him that heareth say, Come. And let him that is athirst come. And whosoever will, let him take the water of life freely." There is all the difference here between a theology which is moral in tone and one which is mechanical, between a theology of grace and one which really destroys grace by demoralising it ; and it seems perfectly clear that what confronts us in Christ is not earthquake, wind and fire, but a still small voice, not a physical force but a moral claim.

At once, however, it has to be said and said again that it is not just *a* moral claim alongside other moral claims, it is *the* moral claim. " In Christian faith," says Dr. Barth,[1] " we are concerned quite decisively with a meeting " ; and when this meeting takes place between

[1] *Dogmatics in Outline*, p. 15.

God and man God fills all man's horizon. Christ does not come as a candidate for our vote, a suppliant for our allegiance ; He comes rather as Saviour and Lord. And the moral meaning of this fact has several sides. It means for one thing that Christ's claim affects all other claims, for it sets them in a different context and it re-orients them around a new centre. They are not simply carried over into the new life, the life with God, like an unexhausted balance at the end of the year. They do not survive unscathed. They are purified in the fire of Christ's forgiveness ; and this is true of them as moral claims quite apart from the consideration whether we would have met them or not, whether we did meet them or not. It is not just our particular sins and shortcomings but even the standards by which we sinned, that are forgiven. And here there comes into view another side to the moral meaning of our meeting with God in Christ. This claim is itself, by the very fact that it is this claim, not just a claim but, as we have already seen, a gift, a gift of forgiveness and mercy. " Come unto me " and " Follow me ", said Jesus ; and they mean the same thing : but, while the one emphasises the practical directive, the moral claim, the other stresses the gift which it includes. But if it is a gift of mercy and forgiveness, then it is also a judgment, representing another side to the moral meaning of our meeting with God in Christ. This claim judges us in the whole length and breadth of our being, not only in respect of our individual deeds and misdeeds, but also in respect of the standards we have acknowledged and the aspirations we have cherished, not only with regard to ourselves as individual men and women, but also as members of human society in the broadest possible sense. If we at our best are not what we are but what we aim to be, then even our dreams are brought to judgment. Most certainly, then, the claim of Christ is not one moral claim amongst many. It is a moral claim in which all other moral claims are

judged, forgiven and transformed. If we take such an
anticipation of the Gospel as we find in Isaiah, " Fear
not, for I have redeemed thee ; I have called thee by
thy name, thou art mine ", or such an apostolic exposition of it as we find in the eighth chapter of St. Paul's
Epistle to the Romans, it is obvious that the element of
claim cannot be separated from the element of gift, the
new life from the new relationship to God, and that
the newness of both is itself a judgment upon the old,
even at its highest and its best. Here again, I find that
Forsyth has expressed the matter well. Christ comes
to us, he says,[1] as " the Redeemer, the Redeemer of
conscience, the Holy Redeemer. Who thus masters
conscience is King of men. He masters man's inner
master." The claim of Christ is a moral claim indeed,
but it is a moral claim which renews the whole moral
world with all its claims and counter-claims, and re-
builds it around Himself as centre.

[1] *The Justification of God*, p. 57.

CHAPTER II

CHRISTIAN FAITH AND MORAL RESPONSIBILITY

THE claim of Christ is a moral claim, but, being the claim of Christ and none other, it is a claim of divine grace which in claiming us is also reclaiming us and opening up before us unimagined vistas of moral and spiritual life, unsuspected possibilities of fellowship between man and man within an all-encompassing fellowship of man with God. In thus claiming us for Himself, however, and for the larger life of His Kingdom, Christ also lays a judgment upon us, a judgment which is as moral as the claim from which it proceeds. It is the judgment that in the world we are already in prison, although we do not suspect the walls and bars until Christ Himself opens the door and summons us out. It is, in other words, the judgment that in the world we have all sinned and come short of the glory of God. It is this judgment which Christian faith seeks to express in its doctrine of sin, and since it is a moral judgment it behoves us in understanding the doctrine to be continually sensitive to ethical considerations (which stem not from some alien reality but from human life itself), yet not too sensitive, for we should see in them direction-posts rather than halt-signs, being concerned above everything else to follow the light and logic of conscience—conscience illuminated by Christ. It is perilously easy to pass unwittingly from just criticism of misplaced theological antimoralism to more questionable criticism on ethical grounds of what may be genuine and inalienable insights of the Christian faith.

Professor H. D. Lewis and Professor C. A. Campbell, for example, have both been rightly alarmed by the fact that the attitude of so many theologians to natural

morality should be one of indifference and even contempt, so that they do not trouble to think out their
theology in relation to the normal insights of the ordinary
moral consciousness, and consequently commit themselves to affirmations which strike the layman as incredible, and which are themselves not always free of
self-contradiction.   " The dominant trend in Protestant
theology today," says Professor Lewis,[1] " is altogether at
variance with elementary ethical principles which we
take for granted from day to day, and which the moral
philosopher seeks to describe and correlate."   In particular, he holds, Barthianism in one way or another
denies that man's will is free, that human beings vary
widely in moral character and attainment, and that
each man is responsible only for what he himself has
done or failed to do.

Thus morality disappears completely from the theological picture of humanity ; and yet, as Professor Lewis
and others have pointed out,[2] Barthian theologians do
not hesitate to use, perhaps in some hidden meaning of
their own, the very terms of ordinary morality.   This
of course is quite indefensible, and it will not do to
despise all natural morality in one breath and then in
the next, in describing the state of total depravity in
which all men are held to stand, to employ for that purpose the very words, and therefore, presumably, the
ideas, of secular morality.   If it is of no interest to the
Barthian theologian as such that, for example, John is
a good son, it should equally be of no interest to him
that James is a bad one.   No doubt the reason for this
contempt of natural goodness is to safeguard the Christian
insight that all men stand in equal need of God's grace ;[3]

[1] H. D. Lewis, *Morals and the New Theology* (Gollancz), p. 8.
[2] *Cf.* H. D. Lewis, " Morality and Religion," *Philosophy*, January, 1949,
p. 4.
[3] Dr. Barth in his later work admits that it is a mistake to indulge in the
extravagant condemnation of man in order to throw God's grace into relief
(*cf. Dogmatik* (Evangelischer Verlag A. G. Zollikon-Zürich, 1948), Vol. III,
2, p. 333), but, as we shall see later, this admission is made in such a way

but this insight does not in fact require such contempt and indifference, and, even if it did, it would be indeed arbitrary to restrict it to human goodness and to insist on taking human badness in all seriousness. If the theologian despises human right-doing he cannot very well raise his hands in alarm and horror over human wrong-doing. If, on the other hand, ethical terms are used by the theologian in some non-ethical sense it would have been very much better if a new terminology had been chosen. Indeed it is fairly certain that in that event a new terminology would long since have been invented and would have become established by custom, just as the Christian faith, in re-interpreting and deepening the notion of happiness, had " to find another word for it, such as the word ' blessedness '."[1]

The plea then by Professor Lewis is both forcible and timely ; and yet it may be that, with the best will in the world, theology, if it is to remain true to itself, cannot conciliate ethics to the full extent which this demand would involve. It may well be that the rapprochement between ethics and theology, if it is to come at all, must come equally from both sides of the present line of division, and that the rift between the two disciplines is ultimately due to misconceptions on the part of moralists as well as theologians. The recognition of this possibility is at any rate the presupposition of any open-minded discussion of the matter ; and it can borrow a certain support from history into the bargain, for it is now fairly generally agreed that the controversies between science and religion of half a century ago were very largely due to errors on the part of both sets of protagonists and to their common failure to recognise the appropriate limits of their different spheres. Equally clearly, however, if this thesis is to gain assent it must

that it raises as many problems as it solves. Moreover, it must be borne in mind that it is Barth's earlier position that has proved the most potent force in contemporary theology, and that his later contentions are to be understood as a modification of, a variation within, that earlier position.

[1] H. H. Farmer, *God and Men* (Nisbet, 1948), p. 129.

be prepared to pass from generalities to more specific contentions, and such considerations must now engage our attention.

Professor Lewis seems to be on firm ground when he complains about the manifest indifference of Barthian theologians to, and their plain contempt for, the cognate insights and arguments of the sister study of moral philosophy, an indifference and contempt so complete that theologians of this school do not hesitate to contradict ethical affirmations without the slightest explicit recognition that they are doing so. Still less do they attempt to re-state these moral insights which they contradict in order to bring out the grain of truth that they might have been thought to contain. Of course such theologians regard themselves as expounding a divine *revelation* which has no need to commend itself to human *reason* ; and yet, most plainly, this in itself is a very inadequate defence. Barthian theologians can hardly be ignorant of the fact that there are other Christian theologians concerned to expound the same divine revelation who believe that, while there may be no need for the divine revelation to commend itself to human reason, none the less God *does* commend His love toward us. As Job has it, " God is not a man, as I am, that I should answer Him and that we should come together in judgment." Still less is it appropriate that I should legislate for God in all His dealings with His children. Rather must we leave the initiative with Him and conform our thoughts to His ways. And as a matter of fact the conviction that God's approach is in some way a moral approach, that grace, so far from belonging to the non-moral, belongs to the higher unimagined reaches of morality, is so persistent, and the radical separation of Christian faith from the moral consciousness so drastic an innovation, that this divorce between morality and religion must be treated with the greatest possible caution and even suspicion. Moreover, the appeal to the divine revelation as providing the justification of theological intransigence and of theological indifference to everything not specifically theological is in the end, and must always be, an appeal to a certain *human understanding* of the revelation ; and it is this fact that justifies the charge of spiritual arrogance which Professor Lewis has preferred. The merciless cut and thrust of intellectual debate is one thing, but the arrogant refusal to discuss is another thing altogether ; and although Dr. Barth has done Christian thought an inestimable service, this strain of arrogance in the movement he has initiated can scarcely be ranked as an asset.

Professor Lewis is, however, on much more dangerous ground when he widens the target of his attack to include almost the whole area of Protestant theology,[1] and when he argues that theology must abandon, for instance, the doctrine that all men are equally sinful and the idea of collective responsibility which has sometimes been used in the exposition of it. What Professor Lewis, then, is condemning is the distinctively theological doctrine of sin in general rather than one particular version of it ; and although he does not say so explicitly he leaves the impression that he would substitute for the universality of sin the widespread fact of moral imperfection. This of course is a fact which even a non-religious moralist might well recognise, and presumably therefore religion is relevant only as providing a cure for the disease. It often happens, however, that the preliminary to an effective cure is a diagnosis of the complaint more adequate than that which the patient himself fondly entertains. Now it is precisely this recognisably theological diagnosis (and not simply, let it be repeated, one misguided form of it) which in the end Professor Lewis seems driven to condemn, and it is here, when he passes from the particular to the general, that his arguments seem to carry least conviction.

There are indeed three ethical contentions which seem at first sight plausible enough but which, if they are

[1] *Cf. Morals and the New Theology*, pp. 41 ff.

true, imperil the full insight of Christian faith that the claim of Christ is a moral claim, is *the* moral claim seeking to renew the entire moral world in which we live, and which would ultimately reduce that claim to one claim amongst others, even though it be a higher one than they, or to one set of claims, one ethical system amongst others, even though it be superior to any other system that we know. These three contentions are that the idea of collective responsibility, in terms of which the doctrine of universal sin is often expressed, is ethically indefensible ; that pride, with which in some sense the spirit of sin is frequently identified, is in itself morally neutral and not necessarily evil ; and that moral responsibility for sin is only conceivable where there is a genuinely sinless alternative available to the sinner.

In dismissing the idea of collective responsibility as ethically unsound Professor Lewis admits that the question cannot really be settled by argument and proof but must turn in the end upon an " appeal to immediate ethical insight." None the less, something can be done by way of distinguishing the idea of collective responsibility from a number of quite legitimate notions with which sometimes it is confused and from which therefore it is apt to borrow the appearance of validity. Thus collective responsibility is to be distinguished, Professor Lewis maintains, from the emotional involvement of one person in the conduct of another, as when a parent is emotionally involved in the behaviour of his son, from legal responsibility for the conduct of others, as when a father is held responsible in law for the misdemeanours of his child, and from a certain moral responsibility towards others, namely, the responsibility of so acting towards them that their way of acting will in turn be affected in certain desirable ways. And, as a result of this analysis, it is held to be clear that while we may be emotionally involved in the conduct of others, or legally responsible for it, or morally responsible for trying to mould it so far as we can, yet in the end we can never be morally responsible for anything that someone else has done but only for what we ourselves have done or failed to do.

This argument is perfectly sound ; but it is to be noticed that what it proves, or at least upholds, is that, like railway tickets, moral responsibility cannot be transferred. It indicates that A is never responsible for what B has done ; but it does not at all support the belief that A and B are never jointly or collectively responsible for a certain action or course of action. No doubt if there is such collective responsibility it means in a way that A *is* responsible for what B has done, but only in a way, in a very elliptical and partial fashion. Strictly, what is true in that event is not that A is responsible for something done by B, but that A and B together are responsible for a certain course of action to which each has made his own contribution. In other words, this part of Professor Lewis's discussion is not really concerned with collective responsibility. It remains within the realm of individual responsibility, and it seeks to maintain that such responsibility can never be transferred from one person to another, and that for every individual action it is always and only the actor himself who is morally answerable. Moreover, this contention does seem to be perfectly true and to be so whether or not the suggested transference of responsibility is thought of as diminishing the responsibility of the actor himself. In either case what is suggested is a transference or transmission of individual moral responsibility, and that is not possible. A is responsible for his own conduct and B for his ; and in either case the responsibility is entirely inalienable. But the question whether, over and above, A and B are together, jointly or collectively responsible for some course of action is another matter altogether. Even when Professor Lewis brings his argument to a climax and re-affirms the conviction on which he must take his stand " in the final analysis, namely that it is evident, as an immediate assurance of the moral consciousness, and thus independently of any kind of argument, that no person can be responsible for the action of another,"[1] it is clear that he is still moving within the sphere of individual responsibility, and that he is still considering within that sphere whether such responsibility can be transferred or not. But, whatever be the conclusion of this discussion, the separate question remains whether outside this sphere there are joint actions for which individuals are jointly responsible.

There are certain points in the course of his argument at which Professor Lewis does deal with this latter problem ; but even here his conclusion is that, in what are loosely described as joint undertakings or collective enterprises, we are still confronted by individual responsibility, and we are still moving in the realm of individual responsibility, for the simple reason that there is no other moral realm in which to move. Each agent's " responsibility in the proper moral sense terminates strictly with his part in a joint undertaking " ;[2] where there are two collaborators " there are two actions and two agents, and each agent bears his own responsibility and guilt ; the responsibility cannot be spread out over the undertaking as a whole " ;[3] and so also, *mutatis mutandis*, where there are three or more participants. " It would be a great mistake to suppose that we have here a single criminal operation the blame for which rests equally on all concerned "[4]—such is Professor Lewis's considered verdict on a supposed burglary involving planners, thieves, accessories after the fact and receivers. More generally, he says, " if I were asked to put forward an ethical principle which I considered to be especially certain, it would be that no one can be responsible, in the properly ethical sense, for the conduct of another. Responsibility belongs essentially to the individual."[5]

Now of course this does represent one possible account

---

[1] *Morals and the New Theology*, p. 87.   [2] *Ibid.*, p. 82.   [3] *Ibid.*, p. 83.
[4] H. D. Lewis, *Morals and Revelation* (George Allen & Unwin, 1951), p. 113.   [5] *Ibid.*, p. 102.

of supposedly collective enterprises, namely that they are really in each case a number of interlocking individual actions for each of which the appropriate actor, and only he, is responsible ; and Professor Lewis has something to say in defence of this position. He rightly points out that, for example, in the case of a crime committed by one man at the instigation of another, or, for that matter, in the case of any joint criminal action, the law would discriminate between the different actors according to what each had done ; and the moral consciousness would in general follow this practice, though it might condemn where the law exonerates and excuse where the law condemns. It is to be noticed, however, that this moral discrimination does not imply, as Professor Lewis assumes, that " responsibility belongs essentially to the individual ", and that collective enterprises are invariably the simple sum of a number of individual acts performed by a number of individual actors.

On the contrary, to treat them thus, to regard the interlinking of the various actions as an external, accidental, contingent and negligible factor is to run the serious risk of ignoring the most relevant moral aspect of the whole situation. One partner's share in a joint undertaking of questionable character may *in itself* be perfectly harmless and innocent, whereas to the ordinary moral consciousness, aware of other facts, the man may be just as much committed to the whole course of action as anyone else concerned, and consequently involved in the general guilt, and only the acknowledgment of collective responsibility can conveniently find room for this insight. Here as elsewhere we murder to dissect. What lies behind the moral discrimination of the ordinary consciousness, to which Professor Lewis draws attention and upon which he lays so much stress, is not the conviction that responsibility is always individual, but, on the contrary, the awareness that where several men are wholly committed to the whole of a joint enterprise they must be regarded as collectively responsible for it, and the moral discrimination in question is in fact a deliberate modification of that collective responsibility on the ground that in one way or another the condition of collective responsibility, namely that all must be wholly committed to the whole enterprise, is not *fully* realised. The moral consciousness may then judge one man less severely than another because, as it appears, he is less wholly committed to the joint undertaking which is under review, or because in his case there are extenuating circumstances which suggest that in an easier situation he might have acted otherwise. Reasons such as these—and these are the grounds on which the moral consciousness does discriminate—indicate, not that the moral judgments in question fall within the realm of individual responsibility, but rather that they belong to a sphere of collective enterprise where, however, the enterprises are only more or less collective. When the moral consciousness discriminates, when it says, for example, that it blames A more than B, it is not at all delivering a number of separate judgments upon a number of individual actors in respect of a number of individual acts ; rather it is breaking up and modifying what would otherwise be a single common judgment upon a collective enterprise, and it is following that course because the enterprise in question is, in greater or less degree, only an imperfectly collective one. The background of this moral discrimination is in fact the recognition of collective responsibility ; but the ordinary moral consciousness does, and must, discriminate, because rarely, if ever, in this or in that situation, are we confronted by a completely collective enterprise, and because, moreover, we, being fallible human beings, can never be sure that we have grasped correctly all the relevant circumstances.[1]

When however we are judged by God, all-wise and

[1] The need to discriminate is ordinarily felt more strongly when punishment may follow the moral judgment than when some form of common reward is likely to ensue (*cf.* the island of Malta and its George Cross) even though in the latter case the enterprise may not be fully collective.

all-seeing, and when, moreover, we are judged, not in respect of this train of action or of that, but in respect of the general human enterprise as a whole, the life of the world which is fundamentally but sinfully affirmed as *our* life, as man's life, these reservations no longer apply. There is nothing outside this enterprise upon which to ground the ordinary discrimination of a moral conscious-ness ; we ourselves are wholly within it. This enter-prise is as long and as broad as human life itself, as natural human life apart from the grace of God. In it the life and sovereignty of man are affirmed over against the life and sovereignty of God. It is in this sense pre-cisely that theologically the world is one world and stands thereby in need of divine redemption. Within this joint undertaking, which is the world, there are all sorts of individual efforts, collective enterprises and rival plots, but they all take place within a deeper unanimity, a human condition to which Christ speaks when He lays His claim upon human life, a claim which reclaims and redeems. So Christ declined to be sidetracked by the man whose brother refused to share with him their in-heritance. " Man, who made me a judge or a divider over you ? " It was not that He was indifferent to natural justice ; His refusal stemmed from an opposite source, from a deeper and more fundamental concern, a concern with that in which they were wholly and com-pletely at one. He refused to be merely a judge because He had come to be a saviour. To the mind of Christ, perfectly attuned as it was to ultimate moral reality, these two quarrelsome brothers none the less stood shoulder to shoulder, and their fundamental togetherness is in miniature a picture of the general human situation as it appears in the sight of God.

It is here that the ethically defensible concept of col-lective responsibility is applicable without modification or reservation, for, from the theological point of view, the *world* is an all-comprehensive and completely collective enterprise, in which, behind all our natural activities, good or bad, selfish or altruistic, there lies the collective affirmation of human life and human society as a purely human concern, to be governed and directed by human thought and wisdom to the glory of man, an affirmation which is no more mine than my neighbour's and which is yet both wholly mine and his as well. This purely human context of life is not just there as a fact but is affirmed in spite of the facts. Even religion and our knowledge of God, which might be expected to break down this self-sufficiency and self-containedness, can be themselves brought within it and subordinated to man's will, as was so often the case with the scribes and the pharisees who had a zeal for God but not according to knowledge. Indeed so comprehensive and universal is this collective affirmation of humanity that left to themselves men are unaware of it and only detect it in the light of God's gracious self-revelation. Yet they are equally responsible for it since they are all wholeheartedly in it. Indeed their responsibility for this is greater than their responsibility for anything else that they do or leave undone ; and the attempt from the side of ethics to question that responsibility seems to fall to the ground.

At this stage the discussion impinges upon the second main ethical contention with which we are concerned to deal, the sinfulness of human pride. For if there is a collective affirmation of human life in a purely human context, and if in reality men are the creatures of a loftier Being, God, who intends them to be guided constantly by His law and animated by His Spirit, there is considerable force in the description of their fundamental and collective assertion of independence in terms of pride, just as there is force in its description in terms of rebellion. This ultimate state of affairs, which, according to the theologian, constitutes the fundamental human situation, is a state of affairs characterised by pride, and, moreover, a state of affairs condemned by the theologian from his standpoint as pernicious and sinful. There can be no question here, on this ultimate level, of a good pride and a bad pride. All pride here is the same pride and it is all sinful.

Against all this Professor Lewis has insisted that the proposition that " pride must be always and inherently sinful " is nonsense. " Pride in some forms," he adds,[1] " is even a quality we ought to be at pains to cultivate." And this of course is perfectly true. There is real moral sense in saying that a man ought to take pride in his work, although this pride which can act as a check upon bad workmanship can become in an extravagant form a snare to good. But all these judgments, although they are true, belong to a less ultimate, less fundamental, level than the assertion that pride is, without qualification, sinful. The former deal with involuntary feelings which may lie on the surface of personal life, while the latter is concerned with a fundamental attitude of the human spirit. No doubt, as Professor Lewis indicates, theologians have not always been careful to make their intention clear on this and other cognate matters. Some have even written with a remarkable indifference both to the convictions of ordinary men and to the insights of the self-critical moral consciousness. But, in spite of this, it does seem perfectly clear that there is no theological interest which demands the condemnation of all that ever goes under the name of pride. What is to be condemned, from a theological perspective, is the ultimate pride which underlies all ordinary pride, good or bad ; and it is this ultimate pride which is identical with the collective assertion of independence on the part of fallen humanity, an assertion, if theology is to be trusted, inherent in all our natural activities.

Indeed the reference to pride in much theological work is not simply metaphorical but is by way of being a necessary description. What is in mind can be described as a universally collective enterprise or undertaking, and yet it lacks the obvious interconnectedness

[1] *Morals and Revelation*, p. 10.

of many actions which is characteristic of collective
enterprises, and it is consistent with almost any degree
of conflict and collision between the actions concerned.
To this extent the words " enterprise " and " undertaking " are inappropriate and, at the most, serve in
this connection as signposts and approximations to the
truth.   What is in mind is not so much, in the last
analysis, a collective *enterprise* as a collective *framework* for
all life and enterprise, a framework which is defined by
its essential reference to man as centre, which is not
destroyed by competition, conflict and even war, and
for which men are collectively responsible.   Indeed
even the word " framework " is too suggestive of something external to man, of that which expresses rather
than of that which is expressed ; and we are finally
driven to use the word " pride " which more accurately
defines a collective and fundamental attitude of the
human spirit as it confronts the task and the opportunity
of life.   It is rightly called pride because it puts humanity at the centre and not God, and it is a genuinely collective attitude because it is racial pride, human pride,
which is not to be confused with the personal pride of
this man or the other or with the national pride of this
people or that.   It is supremely expressed in the Crucifixion of Christ whereby God was banished from the
human world which was none the less His world ; but
it colours every thought and action, every feeling and
desire of natural man, and gives them a cosmic significance, a meaning in relation, not just to this or that
particular situation in which this or that particular man
may stand, but to a cosmic situation in which all men
eternally stand.   This is the meaning which St. Paul
expresses when he says that all have sinned and come
short of the glory of God.

The third line of ethical criticism has been well expressed by Professor C. A. Campbell.[1]   The central

[1] C. A. Campbell, " Does Religion Challenge Ethical Autonomy ? "
Hibbert Journal, July, 1949.

contention here is that responsibility for sin presupposes the possibility of sinlessness, and the implication is that if sin is something for which a man is blamed, if it is, in other words, a morally derogatory term, it can never be properly applied except where there is a sinless alternative to what is pronounced sin ; and, further, that if sin is universal there must confront humanity a universal, sinless alternative, or, at any rate, whether it be the same alternative or not, there must always be a sinless one. But then, the question arises, if it is a genuine alternative, is genuinely sinless and is genuinely universal, how does it come about that no-one has taken it ? Indeed, Professor Campbell believes that human sinfulness has been regarded as universal only through a confusion of thought between two different moments in the religious consciousness of estrangement from God, namely the confusion of attributing the universality which belongs to the experience of estrangement *over against the infinitude of God* to the experience of *self*-estrangement which does not properly possess it. On the other hand, the argument runs, if the explanation of the universality of sin is that after all there is no universal, sinless alternative, the sinfulness of natural man must be understood as a kind of disease, a pathological state, for which men will be properly pitied but not blamed. For this pathological condition men can certainly not be deemed morally responsible. Now there have indeed been times when theology has seemed to accept this alternative and has spoken of sin as a disease, or as a kind of slavery, or even as a form of death, or at any rate as some kind of misfortune ; but while there is force and point in these metaphorical expressions, and while they do safeguard the Christian insight into the universality of sin, they are at the best only metaphors, and they do not succeed in comprehending the other side of the truth that, whatever sin may be, men are responsible for it. To deny this is to violate the insight of faith. The idea of responsibility pervades the whole language of religion on this matter, and if the idea were found to be quite inappropriate it is not merely a word here and there that would have to be eliminated from the Church's speech and vocabulary—its whole strategy and mental approach would require to be radically amended.

In all this, then, Professor Campbell has made important and far-reaching points which challenge Christian faith to its perennial task of self-criticism, or, at any rate, of critical self-understanding ; and they draw attention to an underlying dilemma from which it is difficult to escape. Either sin is a universal condition for which humanity is not responsible, or else responsibility is restored at the expense of universality. Sometimes an attempt is made to find a middle course between these extremes by means of the idea of sin as a psychological bias ; [1] but such attempts generally fall between two stools, for a psychological bias which is only a bias and not a fully determining factor is insufficient to account for universality, while, at the same time, if the agent can regard it as almost something external to him, it may be thought to diminish responsibility. In the final analysis there does not appear to be any valid way of avoiding the dilemma, and the dilemma itself is perfectly sound if it is true, as Professor Campbell maintains, that moral responsibility presupposes at least an implicit choice between two alternatives, that is to say in the present case, if it is true that moral responsibility for sin presupposes a genuinely sinless alternative. The question at issue, therefore, is really whether moral responsibility does indeed presuppose a choice between various alternative courses of action—whether it is true that, if I am to be blamed and held morally responsible for anything, it must always be something that belongs to a particular situation confronting me in which it is only one of several possible courses of action, and that therefore where there is no specific alternative there is no

[1] *Cf.* Miss Graham Ikin, " Sin, Psychology and God," *Hibbert Journal,* July, 1950.

moral responsibility and no possibility of moral blame. And this, let it be said, is no merely academic question, for it is concerned with our moral responsibility for sin. If Professor Campbell is right, I may certainly be responsible for this wrong deed of mine or that, and my neighbour may be responsible for other wrong deeds if he has committed them ; but we are not responsible for sin, if indeed the word " sin " in its singular form can be thought any longer to stand for something real. The issue could scarcely be more far-reaching, for on it depends to a very large extent whether the doctrine of sin is to be regarded as a traditional but temporary element of the Christian faith or as an essential and indispensable ingredient of the Church's message, whether, in other words, it is husk or kernel. It is with this clearly in mind that Professor H. D. Lewis, for example, has complained that so much religious thought endeavours to maintain the ideas of responsibility and guilt without the " absolute freedom of choice " which they properly require, and has found a partial explanation of this " paradox of guilt " in the conservatism of religious thinking. " The religious ideas which have taken shape in earlier and darker periods of society are apt to carry with them afterwards a peculiar claim to be the most essential and authentic versions of religious truth." [1] And he himself seems convinced that when " religious thought is able to mount to the level of our other attainments " it will have left behind for ever any belief in a moral responsibility which does not carry with it an absolute freedom of choice.

The question, then, is a crucial one, and it is ultimately the question whether moral responsibility does or does not presuppose a choice between alternatives. Moreover, it must be admitted from the beginning that the contention that it does carries with it a high degree of plausibility and that the attack along this line upon the *traditional* Christian outlook is a most incisive one. More

[1] *Morals and Revelation*, p. 174.

precisely, it may be admitted that moral responsibility is most clearly in evidence where an agent is confronted by a clean-cut choice between two or more courses of action, one of which he considers to be his duty.　Thus I may be on the point of leaving for some entertainment which I had planned to attend, when word is brought to me of a friend who, suddenly taken ill perhaps, is in need of my assistance, and although I may acknowledge that the course of duty demands a change of plan I may have great difficulty in resolving the conflict involved, the age-old conflict between duty and interest.　In the event, whatever I do, it will be clear to me and to any-one who knows the circumstances that I am morally responsible for whatever course of action I adopt, morally praiseworthy if I go to my friend and morally blame-worthy if I elect to put my own amusement first, but, quite plainly, in either case morally responsible.　It is also clear, however, that the situation is not significantly altered if the alternative to the right or wrong act is not another overt action but hardly more than refraining from the first.　It often happens that when we seem to see no alternative to a wrong act or a number of wrong acts there is in fact the possibility of doing none of them. When an agent, for instance, is confronted with a choice between telling a lie and telling the truth to someone who has no right to know it, he may yet refrain from both by choosing to say nothing on the matter in ques-tion.　In other words, the maximum which morality seems to demand by way of an alternative to a wrong act, if indeed it demands anything at all in this direction, is not some other act which is clearly right but the possi-bility of simply refraining from that which is wrong.　It is plain, however, that even refraining implies a definite choice, although the choice need not show itself unmis-takably in the public world.　For example, a doctor may deal with his patient's inquisitive inquiry, perhaps about some other patient, by simply ignoring it in order to maintain his own standard of professional rectitude ;

but even the " act " of ignoring the question involves a definite choice on the part of the doctor. Similarly, a man may exercise moral responsibility in the opposite way by unobtrusively refraining from some dutiful line of action, by continuing to walk along a street, perhaps, and by silently ignoring the plea of some wayside beggar.

If then the idea of moral responsibility does demand an alternative to the course of action which is eventually pursued, whether it be right or wrong, that alternative need not be another overt action but may be a moral choice and volition which is not publicly apparent at all. Furthermore, there seem to be cases which are morally significant but which allow the agent no more choice than that between acquiescing in a course of action with full approval and acquiescing in the same course of action under protest. A Cabinet Minister may well be confronted with such a limited choice, although he will often have the alternative afforded by resignation ; again, a Christian employee of an industrial concern who is morally opposed to the methods of business adopted by his firm but for whom alternative employment is not immediately available may be in the same position. Indeed, such cases seem to arise most readily in connection with collective enterprises. Even here, however, there is a choice involved, a choice between merely drifting with a majority and, on the other side, following a line of action which combines co-operation with protest in one form or another ; and there is a further subordinate choice between the various forms of protest, such as explicit propaganda addressed to the majority, self-exhortation addressed to the agent's own conscience and prayer addressed to God. (Is not the psalmist adopting the last of these methods, and perhaps the second as well, as, caught up in a network of evil, he lifts up his eyes to the hills and his soul to God and cries, " Do not I hate them, O Lord, that hate thee ? ") But, for our present purpose, it is the former, more fundamental, choice that is important ; and it is clear that

C.C.—D

where such a choice is present, whether it reveals itself in overt action or not, moral responsibility is most plainly evident.

On the other hand, it does not follow from all this that moral responsibility requires and presupposes a moral choice as its indispensable condition. To say that it does is to take a further important step which may or may not be justified, a step which the realities of the moral life may support or belie ; and it is by no means immediately clear what are the ethical and other implications of such a generalisation. One such consequence, as we have seen, might well be the radical revision of the Christian doctrine of sin, and doubtless there are others to justify great care in this matter and to vindicate the demand that the general principle be not allowed without serious consideration of what it means and of what it implies. For, however plausible the principle may seem at first sight, it is by no means self-evident. It is plainly true that where an agent is confronted by a clean-cut moral choice he is morally responsible ; but is it not also true and equally plain that where an agent pursues wholeheartedly, perhaps, a passionate line of action, in the course of which he has no thought whatever of alternative lines of conduct, and makes no choice except of means to his all-consuming end, he may none the less, at a later stage, blame himself for what he has done, if it is evil, and certainly regard himself as responsible ?

The theory which holds that moral responsibility is present only where there is a free choice is known in ethics as libertarianism, and it is fortunate for the present discussion that, perhaps more than ever before, this theory has been expounded with great clarity and with great appreciation of its difficulties by such contemporary writers as C. A. Campbell, E. F. Carritt and H. D. Lewis. The corner-stone of the theory, its essential contention, is the very point with which we are at the moment concerned, namely that " I am morally responsible only when I am absolutely free in the sense that my action could have been other than it was although everything else remained the same," [1] or, in Professor Campbell's words, that freedom and therefore responsibility imply " the capacity for alternative action." [2] The most obvious, and the most common, criticism of this contention is that it destroys what is called the manifest " continuity of conduct." If it is the case that at any time I can choose between quite diverse alternatives, some good and some bad, and that after I have chosen it is still true that with everything else remaining the same I might have chosen to act in a radically different manner, then quite plainly no-one can tell, and no-one is justified in holding the opinion, that in any given situation I shall probably act in one way rather than in another. How I shall act is a matter of my own free untrammelled choice, and any attempted forecast is nothing better than a shot in the dark. But such a conclusion is at odds with the facts, for my friends do know fairly well how I shall act in certain situations, and I for my part depend upon it that their behaviour too will not be entirely unpredictable. My friendship with them would be impossible if it were. Social life as a whole depends upon the continuity of human conduct.

As it happens, however, contemporary libertarians are most sensitive to this line of criticism and have gone out of their way considerably to meet it and to re-state their own position accordingly. As they see it, this criticism is based on a caricature of the libertarian thesis, for they do not hold that every choice is free. They do not deny that human persons develop characters and, perhaps in the vast majority of circumstances, act spontaneously in keeping with their characters. This fact accounts for the undeniable continuity of conduct,

[1] H. D. Lewis, " Freedom and Responsibility," *Question*, Vol. 4, No. 2, p. 119 ; *cf. Morals and Revelation*, pp. 139ff.

[2] C. A. Campbell, *Scepticism and Construction* (George Allen & Unwin, 1931), p. 158.

and it is upon this that social life as well as private friendship is based.   Moreover, even when moral agents do not act spontaneously but find themselves confronted with choice and conflict, and compelled to put forth a special effort, they may still often be acting strictly according to character.   As Professor Lewis has it, " a despot may have to suppress many elements in his own nature, and subject himself to discipline and tests of endurance, in order to realise his own will to power." [1]

> Irksome tasks have also to be performed [he adds] in circumstances where questions of duty do not obtrude themselves sharply either way.   A runner has to strain himself to win a race, a mathematician or chess player to solve a problem.   But in all these cases action is, in the last resort, in the line of least resistance.   For however difficult or irksome the task, we are still doing what we most want to do.

Now this seems an adequate acknowledgment of characteristic behaviour, which is not only a fact but an important one, providing as it does the very foundation of social life ; and this acknowledgment seems to offer an accurate account of what actually happens.   It does not, however, reveal any specifically moral choice ; and as a matter of fact, according to the present theory, such choices are not to be found wherever we perform an act but " are restricted to these cases where our own notions of what is our duty diverge from the path we most wish to follow at the time." [2]   And this again seems to be in harmony with the facts of the moral life. There are situations for all of us in which duty and desire point in opposite directions ; and modern libertarianism asserts that only in such cases is there such a thing as moral choice.   But, the theory goes on—and this is what concerns us chiefly at the moment—only in such cases is there such a thing as moral responsibility.   In all other cases responsibility is absent.

Is this true, however, and can it be defended ?   At

[1] " Freedom and Responsibility," *Question*, Vol. 4, No. 2, p. 126.
[2] *Ibid.*, p. 125.

any rate, it can reasonably be maintained that the case has been argued with logical rigour and presented in a most plausible form. Yet, even so, it raises several questions. For one thing, it means that moral responsibility is not an inalienable and permanent possession, but comes and goes in the course of human life like a headache. We are not responsible, we are not moral beings all the time but only on certain definite and definable occasions. But this is a paradoxical position to which the theory is driven and one so revolutionary for ethical thought that it can hardly be accepted without a more detailed examination. Further, it may well be asked whether the libertarian theory has not proved too much. The contention is that moral responsibility presupposes moral choice and that a moral choice is to be found only where duty and inclination pull in opposite directions. But there are cases, one can scarcely deny, in which an agent's sole concern is to do his duty and his one difficulty is to discover which of several acts he really ought to perform. His choice is a choice between several acts each of which in the given situation has something of the appearance of a duty, and his one thought is to discover which is in fact his duty. Having made up his mind, however, the agent will proceed forthwith to do what he takes to be his duty ; and, in terms of the hypothesis, desire and inclination will offer no impediment whatsoever. But in the absence of such opposition must not the libertarian conclude that here there is no conflict, no properly moral choice, and therefore no moral responsibility ? And yet it seems hardly plausible to suggest that such an agent in such a situation is not morally responsible.

There is, however, another objection, for it is by no means clear that the libertarian theory is correct in denying responsibility wherever a man follows his inclination without thought of duty, and it is by no means certain that the agent himself would agree even when it would be to his advantage to do so. When, for example, without raising any question of duty a person allows himself to be led by some violent desire, the libertarian would have us distinguish between moral worth (and de-merit) and non-moral worth (and de-merit) and he would say that it is only the latter that is present in the postulated case. But is it? At the time of course the man had no thought of duty, but later he may well realise what he has done and he may blame himself, accounting himself responsible. Are we then to tell him that he is mistaken and that, according to libertarian teaching, his action may be unworthy in a strictly non-moral sense but he must not think of blaming himself? It will be but cold comfort if he is in earnest, for it will not alter the fact that it was he who performed this evil action and that he considers himself responsible for it. But why should he? insists the libertarian. What else could he have done, given the situation as it was? And yet the person himself will doubtless feel that the situation, so far as he himself was a factor in it, should never have arisen, and he will refuse, again if he is in earnest, to break up his moral life into isolated situations. Moreover, there is a further possible development in such a case. Even if the violent action is not at odds with the agent's normal moral outlook nor at odds with his moral judgment when he later exercises it on the case, there may come a day when, under pressure of growing insight, he is compelled to revise his moral code, and looking back then he may blame himself for his slacker moral judgment and his violent action which it neither checked nor later rebuked. I should have seen things very differently, he may tell himself; I should have realised the real effect and significance of my actions. The awakened libertine, for example, if he is genuinely and morally awake will not be inclined to shelter behind finely drawn distinctions which, being drawn so finely, not only distinguish but divide the moral life and destroy its continuity.

An awakened conscience [says Sir Walter Moberly] [1] accuses itself retrospectively of its own bias to a much greater extent than counsel for the defence would ever allow. It condemns itself for long persistence on a lower level of sensitivity, for not having shaken itself awake, for disloyalty to a possible subconscious integrity.

Now if there is moral truth in these arguments and reflections they clearly require some drastic revision in the libertarian thesis, before it can be accepted as true ; and it is important to realise that the seemingly unanswerable criticism of traditional Christian doctrine with which we started is itself part and parcel of a questionable ethical theory.

What then is the truth about moral responsibility ? In the history of ethics there have been three main accounts of human action, determinism, self-determinism and libertarianism ; and of these the first need not be considered here, since it finally destroys the semblance as well as the substance of all morality. If our actions are ultimately but none the less completely determined from without there is no longer any meaning in saying that I ought, in a moral sense, to do this act rather than that. Moral obligation has meaning only for beings who possess some freedom of action. If therefore moral obligation has a meaning for human beings, as it most plainly has, the truth must lie either with self-determinism or with libertarianism, or, it may be, with some combination of both. Moreover, it seems reasonable to rule out of court, not only determinism, but also mere caricatures of the other possible theories. Thus, as we have already seen, it is a caricature of libertarian teaching to portray it as if it maintained that every action was the result of a free untrammelled choice and so denied the existence of characteristic action and the continuity of conduct. On the other hand, it is a mere caricature of the self-determinist position to regard a man's character as rigidly fixed from the beginning

[1] Sir Walter Moberly, *Responsibility* (Oxford University Press, 1951), p. 51.

and all his actions as firmly determined by this character. Both of these extreme theories are at odds with the facts of the moral life. Character is only relatively fixed, and although most of the time we may act characteristically all our actions help to form and modify our characters and do not simply emanate from them. Our actions react upon ourselves in a very intimate fashion, and character is never a rigidly fixed quantity (or, rather, quality). We do of course speak of a man's character as becoming fixed, but that fixity is relative and, paradoxically enough, represents at each increasing stage a variation in character itself. There are endless possibilities of deterioration. There is no standing still in the moral life. This indeed is the ethical side of a broader, spiritual truth which Jesus expounded in the parable of the talents, declaring that unto everyone that had would be given and that from him that had not there would be taken away even that which he had. On the other hand, there are endless possibilities of development and improvement, both in a straight uninterrupted course and in the way of a recovery of lost ground ; and such development comes for the most part, if not invariably, as a man hears and answers the call of duty.

All this may well be recognised by the libertarian as well as by the self-determinist, but the trouble with the former is that he restricts moral responsibility to those cases in which the call of duty is involved and, indeed, to only some of these cases, to those in which duty and desire are in conflict. And yet in making this restriction libertarians seem to be in conflict themselves with the moral consciousness. My desires and my character from which on occasions I may act without any thought of duty are not other than myself and are ill fitted to play for me the part of a scapegoat. It is I who act at those times, and it is I who at other times choose between desire and duty ; and I regard myself as morally responsible in both types of situation, and ultimately no more responsible in the one type than in the other.

Admittedly, I may often follow the bent of my desire without any consideration of what duty would dictate, either duty as I normally understand it at the time or duty as I may eventually come to apprehend it more fully ; but later I may reflect upon my action, and if it is at odds with duty, I may condemn myself, and this even if the conception with which it is at odds is not the one that I entertained round about the time of the action but a fuller, more adequate one to which I have subsequently attained. If I am in moral earnest with myself I will not allow myself to defend myself either on the ground that before, and immediately after, my action my conception of duty was such that the action in question was quite permissible, or on the ground that at the precise time of my action I was driven by my desire and was not thinking of duty at all.

It must be admitted, however, that such lines of defence are not always completely irrelevant. The question therefore arises why and when they become significant, and the answer turns upon an ambiguity in the word " responsibility ", even in the phrase " moral responsibility." Up to this point the word has been used with meaning, but in a general way, and the argument now requires that certain particular uses within that general way be clearly discriminated. We have all along, of course, been talking of moral responsibility and not of legal responsibility ; but many writers who deal with the former feel constrained to distinguish it from the latter while admitting at the same time that the two conceptions have something in common. By legal responsibility is generally meant a liability to legal penalty or punishment,[1] and it is a tempting step to add to that that moral responsibility is, as Sir Walter Moberly puts it, a " liability to moral condemnation " [2] or " a liability to blame (or to praise) based on the possession of a power." [3] This account of the matter,

---

[1] Cf. " Freedom and Responsibility," *Question*, Vol. 4, No. 2, p. 111 ; also *Responsibility*, p. 3.   [2] *Ibid.*, p. 4.   [3] *Ibid.*, p. 5.

however, although it answers very closely to the derivation of the word (for etymologically a responsibility is a liability to answer), is not finally satisfactory, for either it presupposes the responsibility it tries to define or else it presupposes a more fundamental responsibility —since moral condemnation, praise and blame are all appropriate only where the actions in question are responsible. The ideas of moral condemnation, praise and blame are not identical with the idea of responsibility, but they presuppose it and cannot be used, therefore, to define it. Professor Lewis himself is clearly aware of the danger of circular definitions in this connection, and in order to avoid it he suggests a " much simpler account." " A responsible person," he says,[1] " is one whose actions may be good or bad in a moral sense. And the nature of these distinctions is not capable of exhaustive analysis but must itself be apprehended by moral intuition." But surely it is the distinction between good and bad actions in a moral sense which is apprehended by moral intuition, and that distinction likewise is not identical with, but presupposes, the idea of moral responsibility. Indeed, moral condemnation, praise and blame are simply emotionally qualified expressions of the distinction itself, and the one is no better fitted to define responsibility than the other.

The truth seems to be that our moral ideas all belong to a form of human consciousness which has progressively clarified itself, which in the process has distinguished legal from moral responsibility, and which uses its terms in a way that implies a further distinction within this moral responsibility between moral answerability and strict moral responsibility. This strict moral responsibility cannot be defined but it indicates the relationship between a self-conscious agent and the acts which he performs, a relationship of intimate, non-transferable moral ownership, expressible in the proposition " It was my act, I did it, and I am responsible for it," where the

[1] " Freedom and Responsibility," *Question*, Vol. 4, No. 2, p. 116.

third of these declarations is exactly synonymous with the other two and does not contain the idea of answerability to someone. Moral answerability seems to refer to definite individual acts on the one side and to the established moral code of a given society on the other, and it seems to cover much the same ground as legal responsibility with the exception of those matters regulated by law which are not the subject of accepted moral judgment, and with the addition of other aspects of behaviour with which this judgment is concerned and the law is not. And of course it works by means of moral censure and not by legal penalty. Moreover, if within this sphere an agent is blamed for something he has done it seems a reasonable defence if he can say that he had no real choice in the matter. If he could not help it he should not be blamed for it, or at least the blame should not be severe. There are, however, two important facts about cases within this sphere. For one thing, the agent is defending himself against an *external*, *ill-defined* and somewhat *arbitrary* authority ; and in the second place there is no final answer to the dispute, for the accepted moral system, with the moral answerability with which it works, lacks on the one side the fixed form of established law and of the process by which it is applied, and on the other side the inner sanction of a man's own conscience. We occupy here a half-way house and move in a realm between the realms, in a realm of broken lights and long shadows.

When, however, we pass decisively to strict moral responsibility we find a different situation. Here the agent is responsible for what he does, even for actions which only a much later, or much more mature, moral judgment of his own rebukes, for, if his conscience is awake, he is concerned not with individual acts and isolated situations but with his whole conduct of life which is inalienably his life. If he is in earnest he does not dispute his responsibility here, for he has to contend, not with an external blame but with an inner remorse.

His accuser is his own conscience and he and his conscience are one.   He may sometimes treat his conscience
as an intruder, ignore it and well-nigh silence it, for, as
we saw, there are almost endless possibilities of deterioration ; but he cannot be certain that this will be his
final situation, for there are, too, unmeasured possibilities of development and improvement.   And, clearly,
this whole matter must be judged in the light, not of the
immature conscience but of the mature, of conscience
not as it is but as it may and does become.   Judged in
this light the matter seems clear.   The law has a long
arm, but so has conscience, and any man may one day
come to repent the evil which he did, not against conscience, but with it, as St. Paul must have repented his
own passive, acquiescent and self-righteous part in the
martyrdom of Stephen.

The difference between the realms of answerability
and of strict responsibility may be approached and
described in another way.   Both are moral phenomena.
They belong to the moral life of mankind, and the moral
situation is itself a social situation.   Morality in the
broadest possible sense occurs within or accrues from
the relationship between persons, and it is one of the
chief merits of modern thought that it has begun to see
the peculiar characteristics of this relationship.   Martin
Buber has made familiar the distinction between the
I-Thou relationship and that of I-It, and, it is plain,
morality finds its place within the former.   The matter,
however, is not quite so simple as this dichotomy would
indicate, and the social situation described in terms of
the I-Thou relationship is only imperfectly, although
suggestively, so described.   In particular, it is apparent
that the I-Thou relationship provides, not an accurate,
but an ideal description of our social situation, or, at
any rate, that within this social situation we must
acknowledge a distinction between parts in which the
I-Thou relationship is more or less fully realised, and
parts in which it is present only in a diffused form pro-

ductive not so much of the I-Thou relationship, nor yet of the I-It relationship, but of an intermediate condition which might be indicated by the symbol I-He.   Probably at all times human life can be adequately described only in terms of both relationships, the I-Thou and the I-He, although it seems to be the peculiar danger of the present time that the former should be swamped by the latter.   In the realm of the I-He we are dealing with subjects and not objects, with subjects of moral claims and counter-claims, duties, rights and even aspirations ; but the relationship, although moral, remains external and falls short of the warmth and intimacy of the I-Thou. In this sphere of the I-He, or the quasi-personal, the individual situation and the individual act seem to be the chief consideration, and a man's conscience, although it may be in advance in this respect or in that, is for the most part only an echo of an external, ill-defined and somewhat arbitrary authority, the echo of an echo, which may none the less be a disturbing factor.   This is the sphere of moral answerability.   In the fully personal realm of strict responsibility, on the other hand, acts and situations have a significance relative to the relationships which they create and support, and it is within these personal relationships that conscience comes into its own, not as an external authority, but as our " inner master."   Against this internal mentor there are no defences and before it there can be no excuses.

Moreover, it is ultimately with relationships that conscience is here concerned, with good relationships sustained by a variety of acts in many situations and with twisted and distorted relationships created in the same way by a multitude of acts done in diverse situations. It is ultimately with relationships that conscience is here concerned and only derivatively and in a secondary way with particular acts in particular situations, although often, if not always, there are certain acts in certain situations which stand out as crucial ones in relation to the history and development of any given relationship.   If we may give a secular paraphrase and application to a religious affirmation, the rebuke of conscience on this level is of the form, Against *thee* have I sinned. And since it is ultimately with relationships and only derivatively with particular acts in particular situations that conscience is here concerned, what moral responsibility presupposes and requires is not, so far as I can judge of this matter, any particular alternative to any particular act in any particular situation, but what I can only describe as an ideal possibility with regard to the relationship in question, an ideal possibility which might have been realised in and through many situations. And at this point let it be observed that the sense of Kant's famous dictum that " I ought " implies " I can " is distorted when it is used exclusively, as it has frequently been used, to limit what ought to be done and not as a guide to what can be done.

How then is the divine judgment to be understood and, in particular, to which sense of responsibility does it relate ? At times of course it has been understood in relation to something very like an established *legal* system ; and when the defects of that interpretation are appreciated it is tempting to assimilate it to the moral judgment and opinion of society, without of course the indeterminateness and the variability that are generally associated with the latter. On this view the authority of the divine judgment is external to the man who is judged ; it is perhaps arbitrary in his eyes, but he has no further court of appeal to which he can go, for the divine judgment is the judgment of the Creator upon the creature. " Nay but, O man, who art thou that repliest against God ? Shall the thing formed say to him that formed it, Why hast thou made me thus ? " Here of course St. Paul has finely expressed a genuine moment in all religious experience and progress. We cannot grow in grace and in the knowledge of God if we are not prepared to trust Him even when we do not understand His ways. But this does not mean at all that this genuine moment is regulative of the final truth on this matter, nor that it supersedes, for example, Abraham's cry, " Shall not the Judge of all the earth do right ? " Here again the matter must be judged, not by the immature conscience, but by the mature, not by conscience feeling its way in the dark, but in terms of the light that is granted to it. That being so, dare we not say, must we not say, that the divine judgment in the last analysis operates through the medium of our own consciences and consent and finally in relation to our strict moral responsibility, so that if we know anything at all about this divine judgment we cannot possibly be indifferent to it, as we may be to the judgment of others and even to the judgment of society as a whole ? This is God's judgment upon me echoing through my judgment of myself, and there can be no escape from such a tribunal, not even a purely spiritual escape like that of Robert Emmet the Irish patriot in his final speech before the sentence of death, in which, despising merely to protest his innocence, he scornfully exalted the judgment of his own conscience above that of the court. Moreover, in this judgment God links me with my neighbour, and confronted by His revelation of Himself in Christ His Son my conscience consents to His judgment and confesses that we have all sinned and come short of His glory. The judgment does not relate primarily to any one situation but to the fact that our human world has distorted and destroyed its true relationship to God who made it, that as a human world it is marked through and through by pride, not the pride of one individual in relation to his neighbour but the pride of man, the pride of the world, in relation to God. And yet the judgment does relate indirectly to every situation in which men stand as natural men, and above all to one situation in which men crucified the Son of God Himself.

It is to men like Isaiah and St. Paul that we must turn to find the last word expressed of this judgment. " Woe is me ! for I am undone ; because I am a man of unclean lips, and I dwell in the midst of a people of unclean lips ; for mine eyes have seen the King, the Lord of hosts." " O wretched man that I am ! who shall deliver me from the body of this death ? " In the case of both it is not only their own hearts but God who condemns them and condemns them together in the same judgment, but in the last resort it is God speaking in and through their own hearts and consciences, and in the very same Word, the Word made flesh, it is God also proclaiming Himself greater than their hearts. " For if our heart condemn us, God is greater than our heart, and knoweth all things."

CHAPTER III

THE CHRISTIAN INTERPRETATION
OF MORALITY

THE Christian Gospel is concerned with Christ and the world, with the approach of Christ to the world, with the encounter between God and man, and Christian theology seeks to give a systematic account of this encounter and of what is involved in it. The ultimate aim of all Christian preaching is to confront men with Christ, and Christian theology tries in its own humble way to contribute to the performance of this task by the fulfilment of its own proper function in accordance with the strictest possible canons of clear, adequate and reverent thought. Theology, like preaching, is proclamation ; it is systematic proclamation ; and, in so far as it is addressed to those who preach, it provides a background to preaching. It is in a way a means to an end, but an independent means which is not determined by the end it serves. It is not the case that that is true in theology which works in preaching. That is to put the cart before the horse, for it is, on the contrary, the truth that sets men free ; and, into the bargain, it is not given to mere men to judge of the fruits of preaching, so that *even if* the pragmatic version of truth were tenable in other spheres it is not tenable here. Theology, being an activity of the human mind, is not determined by the end it serves but is bound by the general canons of human thought and by the subject-matter with which it is called upon to deal, the encounter between Christ and man. The element of paradox, for example, which we cannot hope completely to avoid in this realm, may be a valuable pedagogic device (although even here it can alienate as quickly as it arrests), but that is no justification for magnifying it in theology. There it can have only one possible *raison d'être*, and that is, in a phrase favoured by the islanders of Shetland in a time of bereavement, that we can win no farther.

Christian theology, then, is concerned with the encounter between Christ and the world. That means of course that it is concerned with God's revelation of Himself, but not with that revelation in abstraction from everything else. It would not be revelation if it were in abstraction from everything else. In revelation something or someone is revealed and is revealed *to* someone ; and the fact that the revelation is found, not in a series of propositions nor in a system of teaching, but in a person, does not alter and should not disguise the fact that the revelation is directed towards someone. How well this is expressed by St. John in his well-known text, " For God so loved the world, that he gave his only begotten Son, that whosoever believeth in him should not perish, but have everlasting life." Even his relatively more abstract description of the revelation as the Word made flesh does not really hide this aspect, for a word is spoken to someone, it is the vehicle of communication between persons, communication *by* someone and, no less, communication *to* someone ; and if it were not so it would be as devoid of meaning as " the creaking of a door in an empty house." But the intention of the whole Biblical revelation is abundantly plain. It reiterates the destination as well as the source of revelation. Some modern theology may lose sight of the world to which Christ came, but God does not and Christ will not. The revelation is inherently and inalienably addressed to men. To attempt to discuss the revelation apart from the world to which it is sent is to distort the very basis of theology, for that basis is revelation, revelation not in propositions but in a person, revelation in Christ, and revelation addressed to the world of men to which He came. " He came unto his own, and his own received him not. But as many as received him, to them gave he power to become the sons of God, even to them that believe on his name." He came, in other words, for judgment and salvation, not simply, as it were, to reveal the character of God to an anonymous, universal mind that might be discounted, still less to show it forth in an empty void ; He came rather to deal with the concrete human situation, which can be described in a simple but pregnant phrase as " the world ", and to deal with this situation in the only finally effective way, by bringing God into it.

Moreover, as theology continues to interrogate faith, there is one further fact, or one further aspect of the same fact, that becomes clear, and it is that in coming as the divine self-revelation addressed to men in their human predicament, Christ comes above all, and through and through, as a Saviour to a world that is lost. His purpose is not essentially concerned, therefore, with the brevity of human life, for example, and He does not come simply to prolong it. Nor does His mission relate directly to those things which constitute man's technical civilisation, nor yet to his political life, nor to his cultural activities. Primarily it is with man's conscience that Christ is concerned. His purpose is through and through a purpose of salvation, and the whole revelation underlines this fact, whether with the help of the evangelists we watch the development of His earthly career or through the eyes of the apostles behold the finished work. Thus the entire earthly career of Jesus does bear unmistakably the stamp of a single increasing purpose from beginning to end, and that a purpose of salvation. To begin with it might be no more than " my Father's business ", but it unfolded itself as a purpose which embraced the ends of the earth and was consciously destined to " draw all men " within its compass ; and yet throughout it was the same purpose, the one purpose of salvation. What faith sees as it tries to follow Christ's earthly career is not one purpose being superseded by another, for in no essential particular did Christ turn in His tracks, nor yet one purpose pursued concurrently alongside some other of equal worth and interest, but rather the gradual unveiling of the same self-identical purpose which Christian faith affirms to be divine. Moreover, this purpose was that of the Good Shepherd seeking the sheep that were lost, and to this all other activities were subordinated and within its context they found their significance. The sick man who came for healing had his sins forgiven him. The righteous Pharisee who required no help and no salvation went down to his house unblessed. The one leper who returned to give thanks was made whole by faith. It can scarcely be doubted that when Jesus is described as the Good Shepherd He is being thought of as completely so and not just as that amongst other things as well. It may be true in general that " all the world's a stage " and that " one man in his time plays many parts," but here we are confronted by the one great exception. Never was there a dedicated life like this. In this life there is only one prevailing purpose which St. John describes when he says that God so loved the world that He gave His only begotten Son ; and St. Paul sums up for all time the Christian view of the finished work when he in turn declares that God was in Christ reconciling the world unto Himself.

There is perhaps no chapter in the Gospels which brings out more clearly the integrity, the unity of Christ's purpose, than the fifteenth chapter of St. Luke's Gospel, which hangs together in such perfect harmony because it is entirely taken up with three parables, the parables of the lost sheep, of the lost coin and of the lost son, which are all of the same kind and which all drive home the same lesson, that joy shall be in heaven over one sinner that repenteth more than over ninety and nine just persons which need no repentance. It is in that form that the lesson is stated at the end of the first parable, it is in very similar form that it comes at the end of the second, and it is reiterated in a different way at the end of the third, " It was meet that we should make merry and be glad, for this thy brother was dead and is alive again, and was lost and is found." Who could refrain from joy on such joyous occasions as these three ? But there is a more profound unity and consistency than that between parable and parable. It is the unity and consistency between parable and person, and, curiously enough, it comes out most clearly when the former consistency is seen to be in danger of breaking down. For there is one question which the three parables do not answer except in a very conflicting and equivocal fashion, the question, namely, How do we come to repentance ? Are we to find our own way back or are we rather found by someone else ? On this matter the parables by themselves are curiously indecisive. The lost sheep and the lost coin were lost, completely lost, and would have remained lost for ever had not the shepherd and the housewife come in search of them and remained in search until the lost treasures were found. And yet in summing up the lesson of these parables Jesus seems almost to lay the initiative not on the finder but on that which is lost. Let him repent, He seems to say, for there is joy in heaven over one sinner that repenteth more than over ninety and nine just persons which need no repentance. In the parable of the prodigal son, on the other hand, it is not so much that the prodigal is found as that he finds himself, he comes to himself, and of his own choice sets his face once more towards home ; and yet in underlining the lesson of the story Jesus again uses the opposite language. He does not speak now of one that repenteth as a theologically minded hearer might have expected, but of " this thy brother " who was dead and is alive again, who was lost and is found. The parables are curiously, one might almost say wilfully, indecisive on this matter. The parables which suggest the one answer have the other one written into their lesson, while the parable which suggests the other answer is interpreted by Jesus in terms of the first ! The unity and consistency of the whole chapter are on the verge of breaking down—until Jesus Himself, on whose lips the three parables are so perfectly appropriate, and who not only put His whole life into them as He narrated them but put them also into His whole life as He lived it from day to day is brought into the picture. His presence on the earth was an answer in itself to the question, and an answer which the completion of His then unfinished work simply served to underline, so that the Church's confession, " I believe in the forgiveness of sins," contains a much deeper meaning than could ever be contained in the father's remonstrance against his harder but more provident son, " It was meet that we should make merry and be glad . . ." ; so too that the satisfaction of Christ, in which the Church believes, when He shall see of the travail of His soul, is something much more profound than the somewhat indeterminate joy in heaven over one sinner that repenteth, which in itself might after all have been no more than a spectator's applause. Mutually consistent as the parables are, there is a much more significant consistency between the parables and the whole Person of Christ. The parables and the Person reciprocally interpret each other. Christ comes as Saviour to seek and to save all them that are lost, and not just as that amongst other things as well. Moreover, there is nothing of a specialist character about His mission such as there would have been had He come to some and not to all. His activity is not in any way a departmental activity, applicable to some but not all. If there had been other departments and other specialists He would have told us ; the fact would have been abundantly apparent in His own mission. But as it was and is, there is about His whole work a completeness, a comprehensiveness, an integrity and a decisiveness—in other words, there is about it an indefeasibly *cosmic* character which drives us on to say that He came as Saviour to a lost *world*, that He came wholly as Saviour to all.

Thus, since Christ came as Saviour to a lost world and entirely as such, it is to man's conscience above all that the revelation is addressed, although in allowing that that is so it must never be overlooked that what is addressed to man's conscience is not ethical propositions nor moral lessons, but a person, the Person of Christ. What He addresses to our consciences is Himself.   But it is to our consciences that He does address Himself, and to our consciences in the broadest possible sense, not just to our knowledge of right and wrong, not just to our half-formed characters, but to these in combination with the ill-defined aspirations, the vague sense of insecurity and uneasiness, the philosophy of life and the natural religion to which they may lead.   In a word, it is to our hearts that Christ speaks, and our consciences provide the point of contact for the word which He addresses to us, which is identical with Himself.

This idea, however, of a point of contact has been a fruitful source of controversy and confusion in contemporary theology, and it is well-known that in the celebrated dispute in the thirties between Dr. Karl Barth and Dr. Emil Brunner the arguments largely hinged on the question whether indeed in natural man there was a point of contact or not for the divine self-revelation, and that even Dr. Brunner, who did allow its existence, regarded it as no more substantial than the empty but pure form of rationality which had become filled with a thoroughly corrupt content.   What is important, however, in the present connection is not the various arguments advanced by either side but the presuppositions common to both, for it is most significant that the only point of contact that Dr. Brunner could bring himself to admit was one that had to be both pure and purely formal.   If it had not been pure, it would seem, it would not have provided a point of contact, and if it had not been purely formal it would have detracted from the miracle of God's grace.   This suggests that the point of contact was conceived by Dr. Brunner as much as by

Dr. Barth as something fit to become a part of the com-
pleted work of grace, something like a foundation upon
which grace might erect the house, or even (if we may
try to allow for its purely formal character) as a site upon
which foundation and house alike would be built.   But
this is much too mechanical a concept of what is fundamentally a relationship between persons if it is anything
at all.   If man provides the foundation, and grace the
building erected thereon, and even if man provides the
site, and grace the building and foundation together, less
is due to grace than would be the case if grace provided
the site as well.   But personal relationships cannot be
subsumed under this mechanical conception, and, in
reality, nothing is taken away from the grace and generosity of the giver if a man has hands to receive his gift.
If we begin with a mechanical conception of the relationship between God and man we are very apt to think of
any point of contact in man for the revelation of God as
a kind of bridge-head, in the human, of the divine, and
then, in order to do justice to God's grace we are driven
on a course which leads to the ultimate confusion of
grace and creation, whereas in fact grace cannot become
creation without ceasing to be grace.   If, on the other
hand, the relationship between God and man is firmly
regarded from the beginning as a relationship between
persons the point of contact will scarcely be conceived as
a bridge-head of the divine but as a precise destination
of God's self-revelation, that in man to which above all
Christ speaks, just as on the human level one English-
speaking member of a German family would be the
point of contact for an Englishman wishing to correspond with that family in his own language.   Between
persons the point of contact is properly to be conceived,
not as a point of identity, not as a kind of bridge-head,
but as the precise destination of communication ; and as
between man and God the real bridge-head in the human
world of the divine is not our consciences but Christ.
    It is then to our consciences that the Word of God is

spoken, the Word made flesh, and it is Christ Himself who not only addresses but is addressed to them. Moreover, in coming to the world He comes as Saviour to a lost world, and in so coming He lays a judgment upon it. It is revealed as a world that *is* lost, and revelation thus gives rise to a distinctively theological concept of the world and to the doctrine of sin, of universal sin, in which it is expressed. This doctrine has often been formulated as a universal proposition of the form, All have sinned and come short of the glory of God ; and there is no objection to such a formulation so long as it does not carry with it the suggestion that it states the conclusion of an inductive inference. If it were that it would be ill-founded indeed, for by the nature of the case the number of instances observed and referred to in the premisses would be so small in comparison, would be out of all reasonable relationship to that which constitutes the subject of the conclusion. Into the bargain, however, and even more important, it is not true that my neighbour's sin is revealed to me ; and who am I to judge my neighbour in this way ? What is revealed is my own sin bound up as it is with what Professor H. H. Farmer has called " this jangled bundle of life ", my own sin in intimate and inextricable relationship to the sin of the whole world. The authentic confession is to be found in the words of the prophet, " Woe is me ! for I am undone ; because I am a man of unclean lips, and I dwell in the midst of a people of unclean lips ; for mine eyes have seen the King, the Lord of hosts." What lies behind the doctrine of universal sin is not a long series of observations, whether it be of natural men or of Christian men who have seen themselves as sinners, but the entire revelation in Christ as it awakens my conscience, raises me to faith, and enables me to see myself as I am in God's sight, and which in doing so does not isolate me from my fellows, does not as it were pick me up and put me under the microscope by myself, but on the contrary underlines my oneness with them in the world which is both theirs and mine. Christ confronts me as my Saviour in being the Saviour of the world, and as the Saviour of the world in being my Saviour.

Thus, while the doctrine of sin may quite properly be formulated in terms of universal propositions, the doctrine itself is essentially an expression of the distinctively theological concept of the world to which the revelation gives rise in convicting us of sin. There are of course other concepts of the world. There is a cartographical one, a geographical one and an astronomical one, but with none of these is theology directly concerned. Its own concept of the world is quite distinct from all of these, and it is important to note what it is that gives this concept its specifically theological character. Primarily, it is theological in respect of its source, for it arises out of revelation and only out of revelation ; but it is theological also in its content, since it is essentially the concept of a lost or sinful world, that is, of a world which has turned its back upon God and affirmed itself as self-sufficient. The contrast implied here is not precisely that between a this-worldly and an other-worldly attitude but rather that between an organisation or system of life which is man-centred and one that is centred in God, in other words between a kingdom of man which may or may not have room for God and which need not be a kingdom at all except in much the same sense as that in which there is an animal kingdom, and a kingdom of God in which God is sovereign and there is by His grace a place for man, and indeed for man's earthly life. The contrast is between a system of life which is essentially and in a quite precise sense proud and one which is in an equally precise sense humble. Thus the world is a self-contained kingdom of man in which man is king, but not necessarily a man or any group of men. It is, moreover, a system which is originated and set up neither by me nor by my neighbour ; it is rather a spontaneously collective enterprise on the part of all humanity, and it is affirmed and presupposed in every action that

I as a natural man perform and in every such action that my neighbour performs. It is natural to me in all my thought and action to make this assumption of a self-contained human world ; it is this indeed which makes me a natural man. Overtly, my neighbour and I may be utterly opposed, rivals in business, opponents in politics, and so on ; but inwardly we are perfectly at one in this, and it is this and this alone which entitles the theologian to speak of the world as one world, as a system and organisation of life. In other ways it may be only tending towards system or even moving in the opposite direction, but in this one respect it is morally and spiritually " the world." It is not necessarily affirmed as a collective enterprise, but it is collectively affirmed as a human enterprise and as one which is purely so, in which man is the sovereign measure of its life. It is this fundamental and pervasive character of human life which is brought from the background and set in the forefront in the Crucifixion. The universal quality of man-centredness is there concentrated in a single course of action the whole purpose of which is the decisive rejection of any other centre, the expulsion of Christ from what is none the less His own world. " He came unto his own, and his own received him not." That is the summary of Israel's sin but it is representative too of the world's sin, of the sin which makes it, in a theological sense, the world.

Now the revelation which thus sets the world under a judgment is addressed to our consciences. Sin is something for which we are morally responsible. The very word " judgment " carries with it this connotation, for it is, clearly, a moral judgment which is set over the world and not just a logical judgment which affirms that men are sinful in much the same way as boots are black. More than this, however, when the judgment is elaborated in theology it has usually a moral element in its content, and to say that men are sinful has generally been held to imply, if it does not altogether mean, that men are morally defective.   In fact the judgment has often been held to involve the idea that natural men are wholly and totally corrupt in a moral sense.   Thus the Westminster Confession of Faith refers to the fall of man and to the consequent defilement of his nature, which in relation to later generations constitutes an " original corruption ", and adds that " from this original corruption, whereby we are utterly indisposed, disabled, and made opposite to all good, and wholly inclined to all evil, do proceed all actual transgressions " ;[1] while Dr. Barth's language has in the past been equally strong, for in his Gifford Lectures he quotes with unqualified approval the Heidelberg Catechism as saying that " I am by nature inclined to hate God and my neighbour," and he says that " without the knowledge of the grace of God we shall be unable . . . to love anything other than power, our own power." [2]   There are indeed places even there where Dr. Barth seems to follow a more discriminating turn of thought, as when he says that here man

> is accused without regard for his age or his youth, his culture or his lack of culture, his morality or his lack of morality, his piety or his godlessness—it is Adam, man, who is accused here, Adam and Eve, man and woman. . . .   They have refused God the gratitude which they owed Him.   They have set themselves up as the lords of their life, as if they were Gods ; [3]

but immediately he goes on to ask, " At what point can man's glory remain, when he is in rebellion against the glory of God ? . . .   To be man means *now* to be an enemy of God, and this means to be the destroyer of one's own proper glory."   The glory of the creature is thus not only distorted by sin but utterly destroyed.

Whether this be true or not, however, it is certain that

---

[1] *Op. cit.*, Ch. VI.

[2] Karl Barth, *The Knowledge of God and the Service of God* (Hodder and Stoughton, 1928), pp. 118f.

[3] *Ibid.*, pp. 49f.

the doctrine of sin does not mean this but *at the most*
implies it.   What it is primarily concerned with is man's
natural attitude to God and not his normal attitude to
his neighbour.   That of which the revelation in Christ
principally convicts us is that in asserting our human
lordship over the human world we are thereby at logger-
heads with God.   It is in our relationship to God that
we have utterly failed.   Nor is this some mild accusation
which a man might make against himself and endure, as
if he were to say, " I have been a moderately good
husband and father, diligent enough in business, a
decent citizen, although, to be quite honest, I have been
a very poor member of the Church or no member at
all."   No, it is much rather as if he were to say, " My
whole life could be an open book, and all my relationships to my fellow-men, except—always except—my
relationship to my own, to my wife and children."   It
is not that we have failed in one relationship amongst
others but in the most intimate and precious of them
all, our relationship to God, which was meant to take
precedence over all others and to be the key-stone around
which the social structure might be built, so that
Abraham was ready in obedience to offer his son Isaac
as a sacrifice, so that Jesus too declared, " If any man
come to me, and hate not his father, and mother, and
wife, and children, and brethren, and sisters, yea, and
his own life also, he cannot be my disciple."   It is in
the very centre of our being that this failure has taken
place, not its present centre but its proper one.   " Against
Thee, Thee only have I sinned."

Now it is precisely here that the important question
arises.   Does this failure carry with it a total failure in
all other relationships of life, a total moral corruption ?
It can be seen, I think, how tempting the affirmative
answer is.   Given this central failure, " at what point
could man's glory possibly remain ? "   " The whole
head is sick and the whole heart faint.   From the sole
of the foot even unto the head there is no soundness

in it." And there is of course the analogy of the body.
If the heart fails it is the whole body that is dead and
not just one member. Moreover, there is the example
of genuine conversion. If I really know that I have
sinned I know too that the Pharisee's prayer (I fast
twice in the week, I give tithes of all that I possess, and
so on), whether it be true or not, is out of place, it is
irrelevant. As well might an unfaithful husband take
his stand upon the copper he had thrown to a beggar
in the street. There are several aspects of the situation
which at first sight seem to point towards a doctrine
of universal moral corruption. And yet Jesus Himself appears to hint at a less simple solution, " If ye
then being *evil* know how to give *good* gifts unto your
children . . ." ; and there are the facts, the solid moral
facts of the situation. The theory of total moral corruption has been advanced in ethics as well as in theology,
but sooner or later it has always come up against the
insuperable obstacle that in fact men are not entirely
devoid of good, and even Dr. Barth in his post-war
work has been driven to give a positive content (which
is as genuinely moral as his presuppositions will allow
him to make it) to the picture he paints of natural
men.[1] Their moral interest in their neighbour may be
very narrowly restricted, perhaps to members of their

[1] In his *Dogmatik*, Vol. III, 2 (1948), Dr. Barth has offered a drastically
revised version of his teaching about the image of God in natural man. In
his pre-war work he had held that the image had been totally destroyed by
sin, but he now insists that it remains in a twofold form, in man's relationship to God and in his relationship to his fellow-man, or, as Barth prefers
to say, in his relationship to woman. Thus natural morality is to some
extent re-instated, but it is important to notice that it is so recognised
(i) as belonging to nature and not grace and (ii) as a fact about man's life
rather than as a norm or ideal governing it, although it is admitted that the
fact itself may become more or less obscured (*cf. ibid.*, p. 330). Whereas
in his pre-war thought Dr. Barth held that natural man was totally and
wholly corrupt, and whereas Dr. Brunner departed from this position by
admitting the form, though not the content, of the *imago* and, with it, of
morality, Dr. Barth now departs from his earlier position by admitting the
content, *though not the form*, of morality and by calling that the image of
God so far as the image consists in man's relationship to man.

own race, perhaps even to kinsmen and friends : their
motives when they do act well may be mixed. But,
even so, can the idea be even momentarily entertained
that never in ordinary men has the desire of good, the
sense of duty, the very slightest efficacy in human conduct and practical affairs ? The contention has only
to be stated for its falsity to be instantly seen. And
yet this is what the theory of total moral corruption
means if it means anything at all. There is, moreover, a further consideration. If the moral situation of
humanity is, as it seems to be, neither wholly good nor
entirely evil, it is easy to see how men should come to
entertain the idea of moral progress and of ultimate
perfectibility ; but if they were indeed utterly indisposed, disabled and made opposite to all good, they
would seem to be completely shut off from all such
moral visions. That they do entertain these visions,
that they may even build their lives around them, is
certainly no proof that they are well and truly founded.
On the contrary, if men are in nature wholly sinful but
neither morally perfect nor totally corrupt such visions
may very well be tragically ill-founded, and if men are
ignorant of their sin it is easy to see how they may
further delude themselves and give sanctuary to hopes
which their *total* situation belies and undermines. But
if the fact that men do entertain moral visions of
perfectibility is no guarantee that these visions are
well-founded it does presuppose that they have *some*
foundation, in particular that the theory of total moral
corruption is simply not true.

Furthermore, reflection reveals that the first appear-
ances which seemed to favour this theory are unable to
withstand closer examination. Certainly, the Pharisee's
prayer is quite out of place in any genuine confession
of sin, but irrelevance in a religious context by no means
argues falsity in one which is theological. And in dealing with moral and spiritual matters it is always a
perilous procedure to be guided by a physical analogy.

Here we are concerned, not with physical forces, causes and effects, but with personal relationships, and it does not appear that one such central relationship which has been hopelessly distorted renders others distorted to the same extent. It sometimes even happens that in certain respects (though doubtless only in certain respects) other relationships are strengthened and improved. A hopelessly twisted relationship between husband and wife, a love between them which has turned to hate, may increase the affection of both for their child, although it will hardly make that affection wiser than otherwise it would have been. Even this *spiritual* analogy may be, and can be, dangerously misleading. It can scarcely be supposed that the effect of sin is to make men more moral one to another, even more moral in certain respects : and of course it must always be borne in mind that the distorted relationship between man and God, which is denoted by the word " sin," is significantly different from most, perhaps from all, distorted relationships between man and man, for in the former the distortion is entirely on one side, it is men who have sinned and not God, and in spite of their sin He remains unchangingly their Father in Heaven. The field of human relationships affords no clear analogy to the damage wrought by sin and no conclusion can be drawn from their examination, save perhaps what seems to be true in any case, namely, that the effect of sin falls appreciably short of total moral corruption in respect of the relationships between one man and another. A man who is dead in sin may be alive to his responsibilities towards his neighbour. The worldly spirit is not by any necessity oblivious to the demands of good citizenship : and it is important, especially at a time when idealism both in thought and in practice is by no means confined to professing Christians, that that should be very clearly understood.

On the other hand, it would be a serious misrepresentation of the Christian revelation if it were to be supposed that the sinfulness of natural man is a corruption, even a total corruption, of only one department of his life, of only one relationship out of all those in which as a person he stands to others. The judgment of man which is resident in Christ as the revelation of God is not merely a judgment of man's sinfulness but is at the same time the fulfilment of the prophetic judgments of Israel on the ground of the nation's immorality in one form or another, is the fulfilment, for example, of Micah's denunciation of " scant measure " and " wicked balances " and " deceitful weights." Just as Amos condemned in indissoluble connection a merely formal and external religious observance and an immoral readiness to buy " the needy for a pair of shoes ", so Christ came to effect a total reconciliation which only in thought can be analysed and divided into a reconciliation of man to God on one side and of man to man on the other.[1] When, confronted by Christ, I am convicted of sin, it is not just one part of my being, even if that one part were the centre, it is my whole life and existence that is brought under judgment, my relationships to my fellows as well as my relationship to God ; and my individual failures which are therein brought to my notice and home to my conscience appear, not simply in their own right and not in isolation from their context, but as representative and symptomatic of an unmeasured and immeasurable transgression. I am the kind of person who could do that. From first to last the complaint against me is that I am a sinner, that I have robbed God of the glory due to His name, and these moral fruits of this unrighteousness are simply elements in the total picture. They are not individually measured by the judgment of Christ as the revelation of God. He does not say to me that I am as morally corrupt as my neighbour, nor that we are all equally and totally morally corrupt, nor even (what seems to be true but in this connection irrelevant) that some of us

[1] Luke x, 27.

are morally better than others. What He does say is that we have all sinned and come short of the glory of God, that by ourselves we are all completely in revolt against the sovereignty and majesty of God ; and if we try to confine His indictment within the limits of only one human relationship or one human situation we are apt to be confronted by Christ's own words, uttered in a different but not wholly unrelated context, " Man, who made me a judge or a divider over you ? " His mission is wholly one of mercy and of grace, and He comes for justification, not natural justice.

Moreover, apart altogether from the very varied record of our moral achievements, even our moral standards are brought under judgment. " Ye have heard that it was said by them of old time. . . . But I say unto you . . ." Our moral ideals and our moral standards are convicted of sin, not of immorality (that would be absurd and self-contradictory, and although moral progress largely consists of bringing our moral standards under a higher moral judgment that does not turn morality into its opposite but means that conduct formerly approved is now condemned)[1], not of immorality then but of sin. This is the truth contained in Dr. Brunner's contention that we may " say that in the last resort it is precisely morality which is evil," [2] but as it stands this assertion is false. Morality is not evil but good. Morality could not be evil without becoming immorality. The insights of the ordinary moral consciousness are genuine insights so far as they go, and to deny this is to throw into chaos and confusion much more than the moral order itself. What is true is that natural morality is sinful—like everything natural it is full of sin, permeated by sin—but it is *qua* natural and not *qua* moral that it is sinful. Dr. Brunner employs the distinction between form and content in

[1] As a Christian, St. Paul could say that " the law is holy, and the commandment holy, and just, and good." Romans vii, 12.

[2] Emil Brunner, *The Divine Imperative* (Lutterworth Press, 1946), p. 71.

this connection and holds that in natural man the form of the *imago dei* is undefiled while the matter is totally corrupted. Yet, clearly, this errs on both sides. The content of our natural morality, its prohibition of dishonesty, its commendation of generosity, gratitude and so on, is not perverse, and yet running through it all is a sinful spirit. On the other hand, the form does not escape defilement. Even Dr. Brunner, as I have argued elsewhere,[1] is led to allow this, principally on the ground of the implicit reference to the moral agent contained in the idea of obligation—whereas, according to Dr. Brunner, the truth is " that God alone is good, that that alone is good which God does." [2] Surely, however, man too by the grace of God can do good, and what is corrupt in his natural morality under its formal aspect is not the reference to the moral agent but the fact that this reference is divorced from a higher reference to God. Our natural morality is sinful, but it is so because it is *natural* morality, and even if it were indefinitely improved along its own lines it would still fall under the judgment of God's revelation of Himself in Jesus Christ.

What then is the burden of this complaint? In general terms it is, I think, that obedience to this, that and the next claim of morality, such as truthfulness, promise-keeping and so on, has taken the place of obedience to the claim of morality itself. In other words, the good life has been reduced to a manageable code and the neat order of law has been substituted for the endless ordeal of love. Natural morality is morality in blinkers, morality with its demands stabilised and brought within our immediate compass. In natural morality the finite creature makes the measure of himself finite too, centres his life in himself and in his human world, and so comes under the judgment of the

---

[1] *Faith and Duty* (Gollancz, 1950), pp. 43ff.
[2] *The Divine Imperative*, p. 72.

Infinite, which is, however, grace and forgiveness as well as judgment. The natural man substitutes the morality of the finite for that of the Infinite.

On the other hand, when we pass from morality to religion, from the purely moral consciousness to the realm of faith answering revelation, and revelation seeking to create faith, a new possibility is opened up. The claim of morality is reaffirmed on a different level and is no longer presented in the form of a humanly manageable code, although it may sometimes be mistakenly interpreted in that way. Thus the commandment of Christ that we should love our neighbour as ourselves is not exhausted in a system and balance of claims which make each count as one and none as more than one, not even the agent himself. It is not fulfilled by reducing the importance in our own eyes of our own interests and by raising that of our neighbour's, until equality is attained. Rather, it can be fulfilled only by increasing immeasurably the importance of our neighbour, by treating his joys and sorrows, his needs and vicissitudes, as if they were our own, and, in a word, by loving him as much as we do love ourselves, as if he were one and self-identical with us, because we in turn are not really our own but God's. Here the law is not fulfilled in another law which must yield in time to another and so prove itself only an imperfect fulfilment after all. Rather is the law fulfilled in love, and completely in every instance of genuine love. But the ordinary moral consciousness by itself cannot understand this—although under grace it is only the moral consciousness that can understand it. In the eyes of natural man this commandment of Christ is unreasonable, it does not make moral sense, for natural morality cannot see beyond a finely balanced system of claims and counter-claims. And yet this is so simply because the world of the ordinary moral consciousness is a purely human world and natural morality has no knowledge of the Creator, the Source of its own light, and the Father of all men.

It does not know the divine will *as divine*, the will of God willing to be a Father to His children and that they should be His sons and consequently brothers one to another.

Thus Christ not only judges our natural morality at its spring, in its very standards and ideals, but He recreates it and renews it. He does so by substituting the unmeasured requirements of love for the specific demands of law. " If any man will sue thee at the law, and take away thy coat, let him have thy cloke also." In this injunction, which is also a parable, the law represents not just a contingency which we may or may not encounter but a universal element in all natural life which is yet in some distinctive way human. Law and natural morality are alike in their adherence to a manageable code, but the law of love belongs to the ethics of the Infinite and its requirements defy any prior precise formulation. As a natural man I know in a general way that I ought amongst other things to tell the truth, but under grace I do not know how to love (although love is the fulfilment of the law), nor whom to love, until my neighbour confronts me in his need and God makes His purpose clear before my eyes. And here the change wrought by Christ appears from another angle, for in place of the abstract units with which alone natural morality tends to deal, each counting for one and none as more than one, I find myself confronted by the concrete reality of my neighbour. My neighbour is not every man, but any man may become my neighbour, any man whom I encounter on the path of life. This element of encounter, this crossing of two different lines of life, is an indispensable ingredient in the idea of neighbourliness ; and although this may seem to introduce what is from the human point of view an arbitrary factor, a surd, and consequently something uncongenial to secular ethics, it is none the less inescapably there for the Christian, and leads him on, when he turns theologian, to enunciate a doctrine

of vocation and even of predestination.[1]   And here,
further, the change wrought by Christ appears from
still another perspective, for the " I ought " of natural
morality and obligation is not replaced, as Dr. Brunner
seems to imply, but is overshadowed by the " Thou
shalt " of the divine imperative.

In being Himself, then, in revealing, that is to say,
God and His grace, Christ lays a claim upon us ; and
whether we attend to the judgment which this claim
lays upon all natural life or to the new world which
it opens up before us we are moving all the time in a
realm of moral and spiritual realities, in a realm of
personal relationships in which spirit confronts spirit,
and even conscience encounters conscience, for God sent
His own Son into the world who was tempted in all
points as we are, yet without sin.   The Christian religion
is concerned from beginning to end with a personal
encounter between God and man ; and since it is a
personal encounter it is also a present encounter.   And
since it is both personal and present it is moral and
ethical through and through.   This truth is safeguarded
by the Christian doctrine of the Holy Spirit which underlines and emphasises the contemporaneous character, the
here-and-now-ness of the revelation of God in Jesus
Christ.   Sometimes indeed it is said, in treating of the
Holy Spirit, that the Spirit is the Spirit of Jesus set
free from the restrictions and limitations of time and
space.   It is no longer confined to one section of human
history or to one little corner of the world's life ; and
that is perfectly true so far as it goes.   In much the
same way, however, as everyone's business becomes no-
body's business, this idea of the Spirit as the Spirit of
Jesus set free from earthly limitations may imperceptibly
pass into a belief or idea concerning Christ's Spirit

---

[1] " In the Old Testament," says George Adam Smith (*Jeremiah*, Hodder
& Stoughton, 1923, p. 336), " predestination is not to character or fate,
to salvation or its opposite, to eternal life or eternal punishment, but to
service, or some particular form of service, for God and man."

which would suggest that it had been relegated to some no-man's-land between time and eternity, between history and heaven. But in fact the Holy Spirit is not just the Spirit of Jesus set free in every age ; it is, first and foremost, that Spirit active in our age ; and not just in the world at large but, primarily, here and now, confronting us with its challenge and its promise, and bringing home to us in the present moment the revelation of God in Christ. Thus religion is neither the unfolding of some eternal decree nor, at the opposite pole, a human endeavour to take account of things eternal and divine ; it is essentially an encounter between man and God, between man and Christ by the Holy Spirit.

This truth is written large across the annals of Christian experience and Christian biography. We may think, for example, of St. Augustine, and, in particular, of St. Augustine before he became a Christian, still less a saint, as he tried desperately to break with the evil habits which in a brief lifetime he had so strongly acquired and to respond in obedience to the higher claim that seemed to be laid upon his life. It was not an easy and happy situation in which he found himself, but it was an historical situation, a situation in time, crucial for the development of his own career ; and into that situation there came as one of the factors God's claim upon this man's life. The important question in the present connection, however, concerns the manner in which this situation is to be described. It might be said, for instance, that here on one side was Augustine in an eminently practical and highly critical situation, at a certain point in human history, and there on that side was God in heaven, as far removed from Augustine and his plight as the heavens are higher than the earth, as far as eternity is from time, and that for some reason or another Augustine perceived that the eternal will of God was relevant to his own predicament, that it afforded in fact the decisive consideration. But while that is a possible account of the matter it does not appear to be an adequate one. At that point in his life an absolute claim was being laid upon Augustine ; his slumbering conscience had suddenly been fully awakened and miraculously enlightened, his whole being pierced by something sharper than a two-edged sword, and we depict a pale unrealistic shadow of the situation if we say only that for some reason or another Augustine perceived that the eternal will of God was relevant to his own predicament. It was far more than that. It was not just that the eternal will of God was relevant ; it was rather that it had stepped out of eternity into time and had apprehended this man, Augustine by name, and that apprehension cannot be adequately expressed in terms of a logical relationship of relevance. It was infinitely more than that ; it was nothing less than a personal encounter.

Another account of the situation, however, might be attempted. It might be said that here on one side was Augustine in a practical situation at a critical point in his career, and there on that side was God in heaven who had revealed Himself once and for all in the face of Jesus Christ His Son some four hundred years before, and that for some reason or another it had occurred to Augustine that that particular slice of human history had a lesson for him in his present, morally unstable, position. But once again, while that is a possible account of the matter, it is an inadequate one, for if this claim which was laid upon his life was more than the perception on his part of some eternal truth, it was equally something more than an echo from the past, more even than an echo from this particular past which divided the long stream of time in two. It was nothing less than a present personal encounter, a present confrontation with God through the Holy Spirit.

It is well to make it clear that any account of the Christian religion as a personal and present encounter between God and man implies or presupposes the doc-

trine of the Holy Spirit, for it may readily be thought
and often is thought that the traditional language regarding the Spirit rules out any such concept of an
encounter since it frequently speaks of God's Spirit in
a different fashion, as dwelling in men, as indwelling
and even as possessing individual men and women.
Moreover, although the origin of this language may
properly be found in a primitive and outmoded psychology,[1] that does not explain its persistent survival.

The truth is that it has survived because it safeguards
and admirably expresses several, especially two, aspects
of the facts. For one thing, the fellowship of the Holy
Spirit is a more intimate moral relationship than any
other of which we have any experience. So many of
our personal relationships are scarcely personal and
spiritual at all. So many of them are *almost* nothing
more than external spatial relationships between animated bodies. In comparison with these the fellowship
of the Holy Spirit is inward and spiritual, wholly moral,
more so than any other relationship in which we stand,
more so even than a relationship of fully reciprocated
human love, which is probably, however, the nearest
approach to it. But in the second place, no other
relationship, no matter how morally perfect, can ever
come really near to this one. It is not one relationship,
one fellowship, amongst others, as even fully reciprocated
human love must be : it is the source of all honour and
goodness. It stands above every other relationship, but
not altogether apart from them ; it gathers them all
up, embraces and comprehends them, and fills them
with new meaning. It is not simply an additional relationship to others, such as we encounter when we join
another society or another club. This relationship includes all within its scope. It introduces us into a *new*
world ; ideally, if we did not so often fall away from
it, it would provide a new environment to every moment

[1] *Cf.* H. Wheeler Robinson, *The Christian Experience of the Holy Spirit*
(Nisbet, 1928), pp. 5ff.

of life, a new colouring, a new context, to every act, because it organises our lives around a new centre, around God who has revealed Himself to us in Jesus Christ His Son by His Spirit. It is because of that that in Christ we can be said to be new creatures and *not* because of any psychical possession or spiritual replacement. Indeed, is not that exactly what St. Paul said ? " Therefore if any man be in Christ he is a new creature ; old things are passed away ; all things are become new." P. T. Forsyth said of the apostles that " they saw a new world because a new king was on its throne," [1] and it was because they did see a new world that they themselves were new men.

That does not mean for a moment that they were any the less new men because that was the way of it. They were, we might say, animated by a new spirit, for they had been introduced to a new world by God's Spirit, and in that new world they had allowed God to teach them by that same Spirit how to live accordingly, in love. The new fellowship was so intimate and yet so comprehensive, the new world which it unfolded and disclosed was so much part and parcel of this new outlook, that there was no question of introducing into it the alien ways of an unredeemed humanity. To live in this new world was to love, for how can you have fellowship with the King and Head of this new world and live at enmity with the King's subjects ? To live here is to love, to love God with all one's heart and soul and mind, and to love one's neighbour as oneself.

Indeed at this point we may see how completely off the rails was John Stuart Mill in that part of his essay on *Utilitarianism* in which he claimed the support of the Christian ethic for his own account of morality. It was a major principle of Mill's system that in measuring happiness each man should count as one and none as more than one, and, said Mill, " in the golden rule

---

[1] P. T. Forsyth, *The Person and Place of Jesus Christ* (Independent Press, 1946), p. 161.

of Jesus of Nazareth, we read the complete spirit of the
ethics of utility. To do as you would be done by, and
to love your neighbour as yourself, constitute the ideal
perfection of utilitarian morality." [1]   As between our
own happiness and that of others, Mill tells us,[2] utilitarianism requires us " to be as strictly impartial as a
disinterested and benevolent spectator." Yet this drab
ethic with its ruthless levelling down of human need to
a dull uniformity, in which our neighbour in the sense
of the parable of the Good Samaritan is almost completely lost to sight, this drab ethic is nearly the anti-
thesis of that Christian love which is in a real sense the
gift of God's Spirit and which recognises no limits to
what it may characteristically do.

By the coming of God's Spirit we see a new king upon
the throne, we are introduced into a new world of
spiritual reality, and we are summoned to live therein
as new creatures, for whom old things are passed away
and all things are become new.   As Andrew Young has
made Nicodemus say,

> It is enough.
> Why do I kneel before your empty tomb ?
> You are not here, for you are everywhere ;
> The grass, the trees, the air, the wind, the sky,
> Nothing can now refuse to be your home ;
> Nor I. Lord, live in me and I shall live.

or as St. Paul put it, " I live ; yet not I, but Christ
liveth in me."

[1] J. Stuart Mill, *Utilitarianism*, Ch. II.   [2] *Ibid.*, Ch. II.

PART TWO

CHRISTIAN THEOLOGY AND CONSCIENCE

CHAPTER IV

BARTHIANISM AND EVANGELICAL THEOLOGY

THE conviction towards which the argument of the preceding section points is that no Christian theology can be adequate which is not thoroughly ethical, and so far nothing has appeared to suggest that a thoroughly ethical theology cannot at the same time be equally evangelical. Whether all evangelical theology is also ethical is another question which must now be asked, and which is to be asked in relation to the predominant theological movement of the present time, Barthianism.

In his *Types of Modern Theology* H. R. Mackintosh discussed amongst many other things a question regarding the most appropriate title by which the theology of Dr. Barth might be denominated. He considered in turn such titles as " The Swiss School ", " The Theology of Crisis " and " The Dialectical Theology ", but although he found something to be said in favour of some of these descriptions he finally decided in favour of another title as quite easily the best, namely, " The Theology of the Word of God." [1] Nor is there any occasion for surprise at Mackintosh's choice, for Barthianism is pre-eminently a theology of the Word of God and its spring is to be found in Dr. Barth's realisation that much theology had " substituted the word of man for the Word of God." [2]

The question, however, of the selection of an appropriate suggestive title to distinguish a theological movement or even the work of a single theologian is one thing, while its precise theological classification is another. It

---

[1] H. R. Mackintosh, *Types of Modern Theology* (Nisbet, 1937), pp. 265-69.
[2] *Ibid.*, p. 3.

is certainly clear that Barthianism is a theology of the Word of God, that it takes its stand fairly and squarely upon God's self-revelation in Christ, and that in consequence Dr. Barth himself writes always as a thoroughly evangelical theologian. In this he distinguishes himself decisively from that ill-defined theological movement which is known as liberalism. If the latter may be thought describable, as W. P. Paterson suggested,[1] " as magnifying the importance of the revelation which has been given through reason and conscience, and as labouring to bring Christian doctrine within the limits of the intelligible and the practical," and if on the other hand the mark of an evangelical theology is the overriding emphasis that it places upon God's self-revelation in Christ and upon that, not simply as providing knowledge where before there was ignorance or error, but as creative of new life, as redemptive, if, in other words, " forgiveness through atonement is the essential of Evangelical Christianity,"[2] then there is absolutely no question on which side of the dividing-line Dr. Barth is to be found. He is by intention, as well as in effect, an evangelical theologian. " There is within the Church," he says,[3] " an Evangelical theology which is to be affirmed, and a heretical non-theology which is resolutely to be denied," and he understands his own theological task, particularly in his *magnum opus*, as undertaking " a dogmatics of the Evangelical Church." Moreover, even Dr. Brunner, who seems to occupy so much common ground with his fellow-countryman and appears to differ from him only on what are in comparison matters of smaller consequence, is yet regarded by Dr. Barth as virtually undermining evangelical truth. If the former's divergence were not criticised and condemned, we are told, " the Evangelical Church and Evangelical theology would only sicken and die of it."[4]

---

[1] W. P. Paterson, *The Rule of Faith*, p. 14.
[2] P. T. Forsyth, *The Cruciality of the Cross*, p. 1.
[3] Karl Barth, *The Doctrine of the Word of God* (T. & T. Clark, 1936), p. xii.
[4] Karl Barth, "No !", *Natural Theology* (Geoffrey Bles, 1946), p. 128.

The general theological affiliation of Barthianism, then, is quite indisputable, for it belongs very clearly to the line of evangelical thought. But there are two points that must be plainly understood. It is evangelical not merely in respect of its regard for revelation and even in respect of its regard for the revelation of Christ. That in itself is not sufficient to render a theology evangelical, for even liberalism in some of its forms may claim to have such a regard after a fashion of its own. Liberalism after all is not simply natural theology, which works without revelation, and yet it requires to be distinguished from evangelical theology for which revelation is peculiarly important. The decisive consideration here is the manner in which revelation is treated, whether as an abstract content that is just there, an object about which something is to be done, some attitude adopted, or, on the other hand, as something which happens, something which is done and accomplished. " The great dividing issue," as P. T. Forsyth saw,[1] " . . . is the question of a redeeming atonement," and not even of that as a far-off past event of which account may now be taken, but as something which grace is ever actively bringing home to the human heart. Revelation for the evangelical theologian is essentially active and contemporaneous in its action. All this Dr. Barth readily allows and proves himself in the process a thoroughly evangelical theologian ; but, on the other hand, it is not therefore to be assumed that there is only one possible version of evangelical truth. On the contrary, there are several forms in which it may be presented, and, while doubtless it is of the first importance to know whether a particular theology is evangelical or not, it is also of considerable interest and significance to determine to what precise type of evangelical theology it belongs.

In this connection, broadly speaking, some of the most far-reaching differences arise in the following

---

[1] *The Cruciality of the Cross*, p. 73.

manner. Liberalism has been described as a theology for which revelation is inert, and for which consequently the only, or at any rate the major, activity is on the side of man, whereas evangelical theology is marked by its realisation of God's activity, by its recognition that it is God above all who is active in revelation. Revelation is not something which we discover for ourselves and to which we proceed to attribute a value ; it is something which apprehends us and gives us a value. We have not chosen God but He has chosen us. We know God or rather we are known of Him. It is no more we that live but Christ that liveth in us. But—and this is the point—while these insights are all thoroughly Biblical and thoroughly evangelical, the emphasis which they place upon the activity of God's grace implies next to nothing concerning the activity of the man who is apprehended. No doubt it is implied that any such activity will be, at the most, subordinate and responsive, but it is not implied whether or not it is there at all, whether the man is active or purely passive. In other words, the principal activity, that of God's grace, is jealously affirmed, but the manner of His action upon man is left almost wholly indeterminate, and wide differences of opinion appear when the attempt is made to determine this indeterminate. Is man wholly passive, is he entirely acted upon as the wax is impressed and indented by the stamp ? And is therefore the activity of grace to be understood and conceived after the manner of a physical force ? Or is man active in his response to revelation, in the faith with which he responds to it ; is he active with an activity to which grace has quickened him ? And, consequently, is the activity of grace to be understood as an ethical rather than as a physical reality ? In the light of these questions it is not enough to describe Barthianism as an evangelical theology : it is necessary to determine its more precise character within that general classification. And here perhaps the emphasis which it places upon God as Creator may be significant, for while that emphasis may serve to keep in mind the prior activity of God's grace, the divine initiative, it may also suggest that the work of this grace is a work of sheer creation.

Be that as it may, it is a fact that Barthian thought is marked by a curious intransigence and rigidity. Especially, in its earlier phases, it is marked by an intransigent rigidity in respect of its predominantly negative attitude to man and all things human. In its latest form, it is marked by a like rigidity in its now optimistic view of human nature, a view which, in spite of its more positive estimate of natural man, has apparently no room for real moral standards—the moral claim as a claim and not just a fact—and so has no room for full moral responsibility. No adequate understanding of the movement, therefore, can avoid the attempt to grasp the underlying reason which gives this evangelical theology its peculiar quality, and so to determine it as this kind of evangelical theology or as that. One such attempt has been made by Professor H. D. Lewis who emphasises " the affinity of the New Theology," as he calls it, " with some reactionary trends " of the twentieth-century world, particularly in the way of dictatorship and authoritarianism in general. The tones in which theology

speaks most unmistakably today [he says],[1] and, it must be admitted, those which echo most clearly its traditions in the past, find a responsive chord more easily in the primitive mentality induced . . . by confusion and stress, than in the cultural and scientific advance of our age. Having failed to make commensurate progress with the latter and to respond effectively to the peculiar opportunity and challenge of the present time, it allies itself with the starker forces of reaction, the affinity being especially direct in the repudiation of that most treasured and significant feature of civilised life, the sense of personal responsibility.

---

[1] *Morals and the New Theology*, pp. 97f.

But on the face of it Barthian theology and social and
political authoritarianism do not seem to derive the one
from the other, nor is it clear that Professor Lewis
means that they do ; and it may well be that at a
deeper level the ultimate affinity of Barthianism is with
some more permanent, more deeply rooted, and more
fundamental philosophical trend which itself may contribute to the reactionary movements mentioned by
Professor Lewis. Thus Dr. Joad has referred to the
metaphysical and philosophical vacuum created by one
such movement, that of logical positivism, and has
argued that

> nature abhors a vacuum no less in the intellectual than in
> the physical sphere. . . . Hence [he adds] the popularity
> in our time of such objects of reverence and belief as the
> divine State, the Party, the Race, the Volk, and the Father-
> land. Round these various objects have crystallised the
> creeds which are at once the distinction and the disgrace of
> our age, Fascism, Communism, and Nationalism.[1]

But it is not only that logical positivism creates an
intellectual vacuum which may be filled in all sorts of
unexpected ways, it is also, and, I think, much more
significantly, that it is a philosophical movement which
lays all its stress upon that which is sheerly *given*, that
it is radical empiricism ; and considered in this way
it does seem to be connected, not only with reactionary
trends in social and political life, but also with Barthian
theology, with an aspect of Barthianism which serves
to mark its place within the boundaries of evangelical thought. At any rate, the possibility will bear
investigation.

Now, it is well known that the last twenty or thirty
years, which have witnessed the theological revival in
which Dr. Barth has undoubtedly been the leading
figure, have seen also a philosophical revival which has
resulted in this very influential movement of logical

---

[1] C. E. M. Joad, *A Critique of Logical Positivism* (Gollancz, 1950), p. 149.

positivism, a movement so influential that, as one writer has put it, one of its principal publications, Professor A. J. Ayer's *Language, Truth and Logic*, " published in 1936, has in Oxford since the end of the war acquired almost the status of a philosophical Bible." [1] On the face of it these two movements, Barthianism and logical positivism, have little or nothing in common and seem indeed mutually antithetic, for it is a central claim of the philosophical school to have eliminated, as quite meaningless, metaphysics, theology, and, in fact, every proposition that pretends to transcend the limits of sense-experience. Yet if logical positivism is compelled by its own logic to reject the contentions of Barthianism, along with those of every other metaphysical or theo-logical system, logical positivism itself contains much more than this rejection, and it is not by any means clear that the Barthian is under any necessity to deny everything that the logical positivist characteristically affirms. While he may certainly resent the positivist's drastic reduction of theological statements, not merely to absurdity, but to the strict level of nonsense, he is not likely to be tempted to retaliate in similar fashion by eliminating all empirical propositions, and he may on the contrary find himself in sympathy with the positivist treatment of the empirical realm.

As a matter of fact, one Barthian, or one radical Protestant as he prefers to call himself, Dr. W. F. Zuurdeeg, is to be found declaring that " in the domain of the view on world and man " he is himself " an ally of the Vienna Circle " ; [2] while even Professor Barth, although he does not explicitly consider the contentions of logical positivism, none the less reveals a certain common ground between that position and his own when he describes [3] " the world of man " as that " in

---

[1] C. E. M. Joad, *A Critique of Logical Positivism*, p. 9 (quoted from an article in *The New Statesman and Nation*).

[2] W. F. Zuurdeeg, *A Research for the Consequences of the Vienna Circle Philo-sophy for Ethics*, p. 144. [3] *The Doctrine of the Word of God*, p. 513.

which everything is problematical, everything must first
be tested, and certainly nothing is to be tested with
the result that it is identical with God." Moreover, it
does seem to be the case that both logical positivism
and Barthianism (or radical Protestantism) represent in
their different ways a reaction from rationalism, from
its initial self-confidence and from its ultimate confusion ; and both prefer to be guided by that which
is given rather than by that which may be inferred
or otherwise " revealed " by the activities of reason.
Such " revelations ", the Barthian would say, are not
truly revelations at all ; they are mere theories in comparison with the real revelation which is given to men
and confronts them as something with which they have
to reckon, while the logical positivist would describe
them as strictly meaningless solutions to pseudo-problems.

For these reasons, it will be seen, Barthianism is pre-
eminently, as Mackintosh said, a theology of revelation,
a theology of God's Word, the Word which God speaks
to man and not just, in an ultimate sense, the word
which man speaks on God's behalf. In a secondary
sense it is of course a Word spoken by man on God's
behalf, by prophets and apostles and by the Church
which has arisen out of their efforts and which lives by
preaching what is in a sense their Word as it is contained in the Scriptures ; but primarily, ultimately, it
is God's Word that is and was proclaimed, and it is
this that justifies Dr. Barth's threefold distinction concerning the Word of God, namely, the Word preached,
the written Word, and the revealed Word, and his clear
consistent contentions that " revelation engenders the
Bible that attests it," [1] that prophets and apostles are
" journeymen of revelation," [2] and that always " revelation is originally and immediately, what the Bible and
Church proclamation are derivatively and mediately,
God's Word." [3] In other words, what man says now

---

[1] *The Doctrine of the Word of God*, p. 129.   [2] *Ibid.*, p. 129.
[3] *Ibid.*, p. 131.

in the Church and what man has already said and written in the Bible are what they intend to be, and are significant for theology, only in so far as they echo and are the vehicles of, not what any man has said, but what God says, the Word of *God.*

It has already been pointed out that this contemporary school of theological thought which is sometimes described as radical Protestantism and which owes so much to its outstanding exponent, Dr. Karl Barth, has on occasion been regarded as characterised essentially by the reintroduction of a dogmatic, authoritarian trend into theology ; but such a representation of the matter, although doubtless it contains important truth, scarcely does justice to the facts, and fails in appreciation of the real underlying character of Barthianism. Clearly, for one thing, there are other authoritarian movements within the fold of the Christian Church which stand altogether apart from the theology of Dr. Barth. There are, for example, fundamentalists who accept the written word of the Bible as the absolutely final authority in man's affairs, and there are others who accord a like position to a particular Church or even to a particular preacher, as some Corinthians apparently did to St. Paul.[1] These are all authoritarian movements ; but there is much more subtlety, much more careful analysis and penetrating thought in Barthianism than would be involved simply in the substitution of some other authority for those that are there recognised.

Indeed these other authorities are in some sense arbitrary, and what Dr. Barth seeks to set forth is not another arbitrary authority in place of these, but one that is altogether self-authenticating, one that is completely given and not the subject of arbitrary choice. When the fundamentalist is confronted by the written word of the Bible, or when the blindly devout adherent finds himself face to face with his Church or preacher, he is of course confronted by something given ; and

[1] Cf. 1 Corinthians i, 12.

yet a more careful analysis discloses that this cannot be
something completely given. It could not, for one
thing, have been given to the prophets and apostles
whose words are written in the Bible, or to the first
early leaders of the Church ; nor can it be given to
the particular preacher. Clearly, if the Bible is my
final authority it cannot be, in the same sense, the final
authority of the prophets and apostles whose words it
contains ; and if the word of this preacher is my final
authority he in turn is not a man under authority in
the same way. And, secondly, although I may be able
to give some reason for this " faith " that is in me, my
reason is to some extent a rationalisation, and I cannot
altogether escape the charge of arbitrariness in some
respect (in respect, for example, of inheritance, upbring-
ing, or some other contingent factor helping to determine my choice of *this* final authority). These other
authorities are therefore in some degree arbitrary, both
extensively and intensively ; and what Dr. Barth is
concerned to set forth in his theology of revelation is
not another such authority, but one that is wholly self-
authenticating because it is completely given to us.
Thus while there is much truth, for instance, in what
Professor H. D. Lewis has told us of the relation between
Barthianism and recent reactionary and authoritarian
trends in the social and political realm, it would seem
that the really significant blood-relations of the theological movement are to be found amongst the logical
positivists, the radical empiricists. Indeed it is precisely here that a link *is* forged between this radical
theology and the social reactionaries, for the strength
of the latter was, and still is, in their appreciation of
the power of an accomplished *fact*, and of the power of
a comprehensive system of life which is presented to its
members as a given fact day and night, discouraging
all independent and critical thought. Consequently
there may well be a certain kinship in the depths of the
human spirit between Barthianism and such a social

and political phenomenon as Fascism ; but the ties between the former and the philosophical movement of logical positivism are closer, more fundamental and more significant for the understanding of this modern theology ; and, it would seem, to fail to appreciate this is to fail to appreciate the thoroughgoing character of Dr. Barth's thought. Certainly, radical Protestantism is radical authoritarianism in the sphere of religion, but it is so because it is first of all and primarily radical *empiricism* in theology, if this word may be used to indicate a reliance upon that which is given and not just upon that which is given to sense.

Moreover, when this theological trend, with its emphasis upon that which is completely given, is thought of in comparison with the liberal Protestantism which it is professedly designed to supplant, its greater adequacy is at once apparent. On this interpretation the foundation of Christian faith is laid, not in some rational activity of man, but in the saving activity of God ; and this change of emphasis represents a Copernican revolution in the realm of theology which answers closely to the whole tenor of the Christian Gospel and to the inner transformation of spirit which it works in the believer who centres his life not in man but in God, and who understands what St. Paul means when he says, " I live ; yet not I, but Christ liveth in me." Christian faith is manifestly not the result of some precarious process of intellection, theoretical or practical. The confidence of such a rational conclusion derives from the constant review of the various steps and stages in the argument ; yet the confidence of Christian faith arises from no such review, but from what God has shown us of Himself, from the witness of His Spirit with our spirits that we are the children of God. The whole emphasis of the Christian evangel is upon what God does, not upon what we do or think ; it is not that we love God, but that He loves us, not that we have chosen Him, but that He has chosen us. It is on this account that St. Paul declares that " other foundation can no man lay than that is laid, which is Jesus Christ " ; and the strength of Barthianism in comparison with liberal Protestantism lies in the serious recognition and in the predominant position which it gives to God's gracious revelation of Himself.

It is not of course to be supposed that the liberal alternative in theology has no place for revelation, even that it has no place for the fullness of God's self-revelation in Jesus Christ His Son. Rather, as we have already seen, the dividing-line is to be found, not in the presence or absence of revelation, but in the treatment given to it. For liberalism revelation is an object, a fact amongst other facts which the believer exalts over these others perhaps for moral reasons of his own. As a fact it is given, but, as a fact having the status it receives, it is, clearly, not completely given. In Barthianism, and for that matter, in evangelical theology in general, there is no room for the believer's exaltation of the facts of revelation over other facts. Such a representation of the matter exalts the believer and puts the self-revelation of God at the disposal of man's mind as a mere object. It is not the believer, but God, who exalts the name of Jesus Christ far above every other name. The historical facts of the life of Jesus are, as historical facts, not revelation for us, nor, in itself, is the existing record of these events. In a sense, indeed, the story of the Gospel, like the Scripture narrative in general, is revelation or becomes revelation ; but, more ultimately, it is the instrument of revelation through which God Himself speaks to men, reveals Himself to them, by His Spirit.[1] In the historical revelation God exalted Jesus Christ in that He was declared the Son of God with power by the resurrection from the dead ; but He also exalts Him by His Spirit in the lives of individual men and women by breaking through the circle of sin and by summoning *them* out to life. The presupposition of

[1] *Cf. The Doctrine of the Word of God*, pp. 131ff.

Christian faith, as an evangelical theology understands it, is *both* the historical revelation in Jesus Christ *and* the personal encounter through the working of God's Spirit, and its mark is its recognition of the radical disability involved in human sin. That being so, it is evident that evangelical theology distinguishes itself from liberal theology by being a more empirical theology in the sense that it lays greater stress upon that which is *given*, upon that which comes to us and is not just contemplated at a distance, upon that which apprehends before it is apprehended. It is precisely because it is more empirical in this sense that it holds that revelation creates its own response, that grace arouses faith. In other words, the response is *in some sense* given also.

It is, however, one of the weaknesses of Barthianism that it tends to identify itself with the whole of evangelical theology and to regard any departure from its own doctrine as virtually a return to liberalism, whereas, in reality, Barthianism is a variation of the evangelical theme and not by any means the sole expression of evangelical doctrine. Moreover, the place of Barthianism within the much wider field of evangelical theology may be determined with regard to the degree of its empiricism, and that, in turn, in relation to the manner in which it conceives of revelation as creating its own response. Such a consideration of Barthianism will be found to justify the verdict upon which we have already ventured, namely that this contemporary theology is to be distinguished as radical empiricism. Not only does it emphasise the revelation as given, both the historical revelation and the present personal encounter through the Holy Spirit, but it even affirms that the response of faith to this encounter is in every sense given. There is no arbitrary choice here ; it is indeed difficult to see how there can be any choice at all, arbitrary or otherwise.

And yet Dr. Barth does speak quite insistently of

human choice in this matter, of human self-determination. Since the Word of God is not addressed to " beasts, plants, or stones, but to men," since it is really *human* existence that is determined by the Word of God, then, although " the fact that this befalls it and the nature of what thereby befalls it are not the work of man's self-determination," yet none the less " it is the work of man's self-determination which this befalls." [1] This of course is a more generous concession to our humanity than Dr. Barth's other dictum that " man is man and not cat." Man is here allowed to be a self-determining being, but in the realm of grace his self-determination is within, or subordinate to, the determination of his being by the Word of God. And there, Dr. Barth insists, we must leave the matter. We must not at any price seek to understand this relation of self-determination to determination whereby the former is " overlapped " by the latter. To do so is to adopt the standpoint of an onlooker and allow philosophy to intrude into the dogmatic domain. But this is scarcely convincing unless Dr. Barth is to be understood as using mere words, for example " overlapped," without thought and without thinking. One may well be tempted to reply that Dr. Barth himself has already adopted the standpoint to which he objects, and that in his conception of a self-determination subordinate to, and overlapped by, determination by the Word of God he himself has harnessed philosophy to the service of dogmatics, and a very questionable philosophy at that. To this, however, he might conceivably reply that his endeavour is to be true to the self-revelation of the one living and true God who cannot be measured by anything that He has made, and that dogmatics cannot properly be made subject to the general standards of philosophical truth. All other determinations of man's freedom might destroy that freedom ; this determination does not. And while there may well be differ-

[1] *The Doctrine of the Word of God*, p. 230.

ences of opinion regarding the effectiveness of this reply,
it is clear that the final understanding and estimation
of Dr. Barth's theology must be within the realm of
dogmatics itself, that is, in connection with his understanding of the determination of man's being by the
Word of God, and in connection with his conception
of the manner in which grace creates faith and in which
the response to revelation is *given* with the revelation.

On this point, as we have seen, the Barthian contention is that the response of faith is utterly given, and in
this sense Barthian theology proves itself to be radical
empiricism in theology.   The Word of God does not
presuppose anything in man but brings " the radical
criticism of his entire present reality." [1]   That it is man
that is addressed is a purely contingent fact,[2] and man's
response is " a quite inconceivable *novum* in direct contrast to all his ability and capacity," [3] being imported,
lent and given to him.   In other words, it is, so far as
man is concerned, a *creatio ex nihilo*.   But this, it must
be submitted, is an inadequate and distorted representation of what justifies the Christian man or woman in
giving thanks to God for the gift of faith.   Faith is
certainly the gift of God and the creation of His grace,
but that does not of course imply a *creatio ex nihilo*.
There are other ways in which it may be conceived,
according as a surgeon makes the blind eye see, as a
wandering star is brought within the pull of another
and becomes its planet and produces life, and, above
all, as a creative encounter of persons.   In following the
first rather than the fourth of these conceptions Barthianism has so stressed the newness of the Christian man
that it has altogether lost touch with the notion of
transformation.   It has forgotten, it seems, that it is
out of weakness, not out of nothing that we are made
strong.

The truth is that, in spite of the attempt to fence off

---

[1] *The Doctrine of the Word of God*, p. 221.
[2] *Ibid.*, p. 221.   [3] *Ibid.*, p. 222.

dogmatics from philosophical considerations, it is a case of closing the stable-door when the horse is out—or in— for the creativity of God's Word has already been arbitrarily subordinated to the sub-moral, mechanical category of determinism. That being so, it is no surprise to find Dr. Barth concluding his section on the knowability of the Word of God with a remarkable sentence.

> It is quite true [he says] [1] that a man must open the door to Him (Revelation iii, 20), but even the fact of that event is, *quoad actum* and *quoad potentiam*, the work of the Christ who stands outside. So that the other thing also remains unreservedly true that the risen Christ passes through closed doors (John xx, 19f.).

But to assimilate and confuse the material doors of men's houses with the moral and spiritual doors of their hearts is utterly repugnant to the revelation in Jesus Christ, not only to the Christ who stands at the door and knocks, but to Him also who weeps over the city of Jerusalem because it refuses to give heed. Confronted by human obduracy Christ is by no means powerless, but His resources are the spiritual resources of love— unless the narrative of His temptation, and indeed of all His teaching, is to be deprived of its meaning.

The conclusion then seems clear, not only that Barthianism is radical empiricism in theology as logical positivism is in philosophy, but also that, perhaps in likeness again to its philosophical kinsman, it is an anti-rationalist protest which forsakes the truths as well as the errors of rationalism and inevitably overreaches itself. Dr. Barth has done well to recall his contemporaries to the broad lines of evangelical truth ; but it is error on his part to identify that truth with his own particular conception of it.

Certainly it is by grace that we can know God and be brought into a saving fellowship with Him. It is by

[1] *Ibid.*, p. 283.

grace and by grace alone. It is all of grace ; and the
recognition that that is so is the mark of a truly evangelical theology. But to say this is to say absolutely
nothing about *how* grace works, about the manner of
its working, whether as a physical force or as a moral
person, whether in the last resort the Holy Spirit is It
or He. In a rather different connection, with regard
not to the manner of God's working but with reference
to the manner of our obedience in pastoral work, teaching, preaching and theology, Dr. Barth has dealt vigorously with this question of " How ? ". " But what of
the How ? I reply : assuming that we had put our
hands to the plough, could we look back ? Assuming
we were really caught by the What, *i.e.* arrested by that
command, by the knowledge of that limit and that
hope, by the knowledge of that victorious power, by
the necessity of that confidence, conditioned by the
activity of that love and perseverance—could we even
for a moment seek the How outside the What ? Could it,
even for a moment, become a ' decisive ' question for us ? "[1]
It is, however, clear that Dr. Barth would give a similar
reply to the present question of the How. "Could we
even for a moment seek the How outside the What ? "
And yet that is what he himself has done, imposing upon
the revelation a determinism which it will not sanction ;
and although he has here and there allowed that there is
self-determination within the complete determination by
God's Word and that we must simply leave the matter
there, to do so is to make an admission uncongenial
to the rest of his theology. It is, moreover, to pay only
lip-service to the notion of moral responsibility and
self-determination, and it is to state a serious problem
while rejecting beforehand every attempt to solve it.
Nor is this the accidental implication of a single expression of Dr. Barth's views, for in a later work he speaks,
not indeed of a self-determination overlapped by the
divine determination of man's being, but of the human

[1] " No ! ", *Natural Theology*, p. 126.

reason involved in faith as completely determined by its divine object.[1]

Dr. Barth has done great service to Christian theology in insisting that God is subject and not object, but we do less than justice to this truth when we attribute to God a manner of working which would be inappropriate even to the creaturely subjects that we are. Radical Protestantism has laid great stress upon the fact that God is Creator, and doubtless it has done so to emphasise that He is subject, that He is the living God in comparison with whom we are only creatures ; but in making this emphasis it may be led, and indeed has been led, to regard God as fundamentally Creator in *all* His relationships to men. Indeed it has inverted the true order to be found in the revelation itself. Creation by itself is not grace, but is only seen to be grace retrospectively in the light of the Gospel and its grace, from the standpoint, that is to say, of a creature who has been called into living fellowship with God his Creator. But in Barthianism this order is reversed, and the grace of the Gospel present in Jesus Christ is interpreted in terms of a sheerly postulated, prior grace of creation.

While, then, the Barthian theology is genuinely evangelical theology, it requires a further and more precise classification, and is manifestly not to be identified with the whole of evangelical theology. It is certainly not an ethical evangelical theology. Indeed the concept of moral responsibility never appears in Dr. Barth's theological system as more than an island lying off the continent of his more characteristic thought, and it is elsewhere that the student must look for the peculiar motif of the school. For, while, like all evangelical theology, Barthianism is rightly empirical, it appears as radical empiricism in theology, as logical positivism is in philosophy, and it does so in respect of its characteristic teaching that faith is *absolutely* given, is *absolutely* the *creation* of grace. If, however, this emphasis is traced

[1] *Cf. Dogmatics in Outline,* p. 24.

back to a sheer assumption concerning the manner in which the Creator will deal with His creatures, Barthianism stands forth as a metaphysical evangelical theology, as an evangelical theology coloured and governed by a metaphysical preconception concerning the relationship between creatures and their Creator. But, even if this metaphysical preconception should prove an ultimate spring of its characteristic teaching, its appeal may well still derive from its radical empiricism.

CHAPTER V

TOWARDS A MORE ETHICAL
EVANGELICAL THEOLOGY

IT is a notable and significant fact that of the theologians who have learned much from the teaching of Professor Karl Barth and have been greatly influenced by his theology, those who have shown the keenest interest in ethics, politics and, in the most general sense, practical philosophy, have been impelled at one point or another to make a stand against him. This is pre-eminently so in the case of Professor Emil Brunner and of Professor Reinhold Niebuhr, whose publications witness, even in their titles,[1] to their practical interest and insight, and whose considered positions reveal decisive departures from that of Dr. Barth. But this fact is significant as well as interesting, because it is no coincidence. Rather it reveals that underlying the movement away from Barth by those closest to him there is at bottom, in spite of the highly abstract form in which the divergence is sometimes stated, a desire and a search for a more ethical evangelical theology, a theological presentation of the Gospel which does not violate, not indeed the moral realm to which the Gospel is sent, but the larger moral realm to which it belongs, the realm of God's grace summoning man to salvation.

It is well known that, although Dr. Brunner and Dr. Barth seem to have so much in common in their systems of thought and in their theological standpoints, differences appeared between them and, as early as 1934, were given vigorous expression in two pamphlets published

---

[1] *Cf.* Emil Brunner, *The Divine Imperative* (Lutterworth Press, 1946) and *Christianity and Civilisation*, 2 vols. (Nisbet, 1948–49) ; and Reinhold Niebuhr, *Moral Man and Immoral Society* (Scribner, 1932), *An Interpretation of Christian Ethics* (S.C.M. Press, 1936) and *Faith and History* (Nisbet, 1949).

respectively under the titles *Natur und Gnade* and *Nein*. In the former of these, having warmly acknowledged his own debt to Dr. Barth and the very considerable extent of their continuing agreement, Dr. Brunner stated six precise points to which, he said, Dr. Barth adhered, and over against them maintained six corresponding points of his own, which together provide a convenient summary of the issue which developed between them. Indeed these six points can be further reduced to two fundamental positions upon which the others seem to depend. First, whereas Dr. Barth held that the *imago dei* in man had been utterly and completely destroyed by sin so that absolutely nothing remained of it, Dr. Brunner believed, and in fact still believes, that that is true only of the *imago* as materially conceived, but that formally, as meaning that man is a subject and is responsible, it remains quite intact and is " not in the least touched." Secondly, whereas for Dr. Barth there was, and is, only one revelation of God, " the one complete revelation in Christ," for Dr. Brunner there was, and is, also a general revelation in creation, although this can only be truly understood by " the man who stands within the revelation in Christ " and by itself it cannot bring the sinner to salvation, it " is not sufficient in order to know God in such a way that this knowledge brings salvation " to the sinner.

With regard to these deviations from original Barthianism, there are two main questions which arise : in the first place a question concerning the reason for them, the purpose they are intended to serve, and, in the second place, a question regarding their success or failure in serving this purpose. With regard to the first question it is interesting to discover that in a sense both are intended to serve the same purpose, that of restoring reality, moral and personal reality, to the object of God's grace, and so, we may suppose, of representing grace once again as grace and not as the *creatio ex nihilo* which in Dr. Barth's hands it had virtually become. But this general purpose can be

made specific in two ways, each of which corresponds to
one of Dr. Brunner's amendments.   For one thing a
moral and personal being is a subject and man is a subject.   " Not even as a sinner does he cease to be one with
whom one can speak, with whom therefore also God can
speak." [1]   This fact that man is a subject is the formal
imago dei which provides " a point of contact for the
divine grace of redemption," [2] but, Dr. Brunner is careful
to add, " it is the purely formal possibility of his being
addressed."   " This receptivity says nothing as to his
acceptance or rejection of the Word of God," [3] and, Dr.
Brunner might also have said, it carries no implication
whatsoever that that Word, the Word of God, will be
spoken.   Yet even so Dr. Barth at this stage in the
development of his thought is scornful of this admission.

> Would not theology and the Church dishonour man if
> they addressed him, not because he *has been addressed* but
> because he *can be addressed* ?   By so doing they would ques-
> tion or even deny the one all-important positive good thing
> that can be said about him." [4]

But this is just not so.   Dr. Brunner does not suggest
for a moment that the Church should address man
" because he can be addressed."   After all, God does
not address him " because he can be addressed " but of
His own free and sovereign grace ; yet it remains man
whom He freely chooses to address, and address in the
way He does, because he can be addressed.   Indeed the
only question is whether Dr. Brunner has gone far
enough.   Is it to a purely formal " capacity for words "
that God sends His own Son, or even to this in combination with a wholly corrupted content ?   Is it not to
beings of some moral understanding, however perverted
and misdirected that understanding is by sin ?   And, in
any case, in talking of a pure form filled by a totally corrupt content is not Dr. Brunner simply adding one

---

[1] " Nature and Grace," *Natural Theology*, p. 23.   [2] *Ibid.*, p. 31.
[3] *Ibid.*, p. 31.   [4] " No ! ", *Natural Theology*, p. 127.

abstraction to another and failing to reach the men and women, the world which God so loved ?

The specific purpose served by Dr. Brunner's other concession is explicitly acknowledged by him in an important passage in his later book, *Revelation and Reason.*

> The fundamental significance of the revelation in Creation [he says there] [1] is this : that through it man as man is *person*, a responsible being, a being related to God, " standing before " Him ; and also that by this revelation man is responsible for his sin, and is therefore " inexcusable." This is why it is the presupposition of the saving revelation in Jesus Christ, although in itself it has no saving significance. Finally, this revelation is significant, not only as a presupposition, but also in its relation to the revelation of God in Christ. The man whose eyes have been opened by the particular historical Word of God is now once more able to see what God shows us in His revelation in the Creation. As we know, men might have seen it all along : the fact that they did not do so was due to their incomprehensible, sinful blindness. It was due to man's sin that the meaning was concealed from him ; the result is that man either does not perceive this evident, divine revelation, or, if he thinks he perceives it, he falls into gross errors and misunderstandings. Through faith in Jesus Christ, however, not only this blindness but this guilt is removed—or at least the process of removal has begun. The eyes which had been blind begin to see again.

In other words, Dr. Brunner is compelled to make this admission to safeguard man's responsibility for his sin which disappears completely from a race in which the *imago dei* has been wholly destroyed in every way. And once again the only question is whether Dr. Brunner succeeds in this aim. For, although sin does not destroy " this perceptibility of God in His works," [2] " sin makes man blind for what is visibly set before our eyes " ; [3] " the revelation in creation is not sufficient in order to know God in such a way that this knowledge brings salvation " ; [4] " sin dulls man's sight so much that instead

---

[1] *Revelation and Reason* (S.C.M. Press, 1947), p. 76.
[2] " Nature and Grace," *Natural Theology*, p. 25.
[3] *Ibid.*, p. 25.   [4] *Ibid.*, p. 26.

of God he ' knows ' or ' fancies ' gods." [1]   But what kind
of revelation of God is this which does not save ?   What
kind of revelation is this which reveals-something but
which at the same time reveals-nothing-to-anyone, like
a flash of lightning in a blinded world ?   Is not this again
in a different way a pure form and a wholly corrupt content ?   Is it not once again a completely unreal abstraction ?   And, moreover, if the knowledge is insufficient
to bring sinful men, who have never been anything else
but sinful, to God, are they any more responsible for their
sin than they would have been had there never been
such a revelation ?

Thus it is very doubtful whether Dr. Brunner has
departed far enough from Dr. Barth to present in his
theology the Christian Gospel, and to present it in a way
which does not violate the Gospel it seeks to present.
But, if his final position is most unstable, the direction in
which he moves is even more significant, for, clearly, Dr.
Brunner's aim is to achieve a more ethical evangelical
theology than Dr. Barth's, one which does greater justice
to the moral realities of the situation in which a man
finds himself when he is confronted by the Word made
flesh.   But if this is true of Dr. Brunner's thought it is
likely to prove even more applicable to Professor Niebuhr's.   For one thing, while Brunner minimises the
differences between himself and Barth and suggests
that they constitute largely a " misunderstanding " and
a " dispute about words ", Niebuhr regards himself
as further removed from Barth than Brunner has
ever been.   Moreover, the gap between Niebuhr and
Barth visibly widens as the former's thought develops,
whereas, on the whole, Brunner's position with regard to Barth remains almost rigidly fixed.   In
turning, then, to some consideration of the American
theologian's work, we may expect to see more clearly
the direction of the movement away from Barth, for
we may expect to see that movement itself in motion.

[1] " Nature and Grace," *Natural Theology*, p. 26.

In fact we shall see that still more plainly if we pay attention to Niebuhr's contributions to political and practical philosophy as well as to his more strictly theological writings.

For more than twenty years Dr. Reinhold Niebuhr has occupied with distinction a chair in Union Theological Seminary, New York, and during that time he has made many substantial and weighty contributions both to political and to religious thought, not least in his Gifford Lectures delivered in Edinburgh on the eve of the War, under the title *The Nature and Destiny of Man*. It is not to be supposed of course that during this fruitful period of intellectual work Professor Niebuhr has succeeded in maintaining, or has even tried [1] to maintain, a single self-consistent standpoint. On the contrary, his interests are too wide for that, and there have in fact been considerable developments and changes, although the identity of the thinker is generally apparent from a good deal more than the name which appears on the different title-pages. But the changes themselves are interesting and the detection of their direction a matter of some importance.

In 1939, just prior to the delivery of Dr. Niebuhr's Gifford Lectures, Principal John Baillie was able to describe him as a critic of liberalism, but a critic of a very individual and discriminating kind. " Theologically," he said, " Niebuhr is indebted to Karl Barth, politically and socially to Karl Marx." But, although that was an apt and fair estimate at the time, it scarcely represents the impression which Professor Niebuhr leaves today upon the contemporary mind. Much has happened since the year of grace 1939, and, like many other things, Dr. Niebuhr's thought has undergone considerable change. Certainly there has been no obvious *volte face*, but there have been changes of emphasis ; and in what

[1] *Cf.* his own complaint that another writer had allowed history to add so little to his insights of twenty years before ! *Interpretation of Christian Ethics*, p. 184.

follows the argument will seek to suggest, and to offer some considerations in defence of, four propositions, namely (i) that in social and political philosophy Dr. Niebuhr has moved farther away from Marx ; (ii) that in theology he has moved farther away from Dr. Barth ; (iii) that his theology and his social and political philosophy have become more closely integrated the one to the other ; and (iv) that in the result his theology has perhaps acquired a clearer position of precedence over his political philosophy than was the case at an earlier stage.

In the first place, then, some consideration is due to Dr. Niebuhr's political philosophy. In 1932 he published a book entitled *Moral Man and Immoral Society*, and in it he defended the thesis, against all forms of liberalism religious and secular, that of necessity society is much more immoral than the individual, that the action of any society contains much more " unrestrained egoism " than need be seen in individual action, and further that " this distinction justifies and necessitates political policies which a purely individualistic ethic must always find embarrassing." [1]   In other words, since any social and political action inevitably involves in very large measure the exercise of egoistic power, the inhibitions we may have in regard to such exercise, inhibitions which perhaps normally we regard as moral, are not moral at all ; and policies which, from the standpoint of an individualistic ethic, we tend to regard as indefensible may in fact be completely justifiable and indeed necessary. Even the policy of revolution and violence may be in that case, and Dr. Niebuhr devotes a chapter to the examination of its potentialities. His treatment yields no more than tentative conclusions, but, on the whole, he tends to favour evolution rather than revolution, although he declares that " if violence can be justified at all, its terror must have the tempo of a surgeon's skill and healing must follow quickly upon its wounds." [2]

[1] *Moral Man and Immoral Society* (Scribner, 1932), p. xi.   [2] *Ibid.*, p. 220.

If, however, Dr. Niebuhr is somewhat inconclusive on the question of method, how does he stand in respect of the end which the method is designed to achieve ?   In the answer to this question there are two parts, for, although on the one hand Dr. Niebuhr disavows the ultimate end of anarchism, that is, peace and justice without law and force, and declares [1] that in actual history the perpetual dream of peace and brotherhood is incapable of realisation, on the other hand, he accepts, with certain qualifications, as a proximate and practical goal, the Marxist proletarian's social vision of an equalitarian society.   " ' From each according to his ability, to each according to his needs,' is," he says,[2] " indeed an ideal which is . . . impossible of consistent application in the complexities of society . . . but it is an ideal toward which a rational society must move."

Clearly there is one peculiar feature of Dr. Niebuhr's thought at this earlier stage, for one might well have expected him to see that, if egoistic power is necessary to overcome injustice, it is equally bound to create injustice in other forms.   Indeed it is odd that, believing society to be so much less moral than the individual, he should yet seek to concentrate power in the very hands of society.   And, as a matter of fact, one finds that in a later book Dr. Niebuhr complains that the pessimism which prompts and justifies the policy of investing the state with uncontrolled power is not consistent, " for it is not applied, as it should be, to the ruler." [3]   He favours now the " democratic techniques of a free society " which " place checks upon the power of the ruler and administrator and thus prevent it from being vexatious." [4]   But there is a complication which blunts the edge of this confession, for in Dr. Niebuhr's terminology Marxism does not rank as undemocratic.   On the contrary, it is regarded as radical democracy, as distinct

---

[1] Cf. Moral Man and Immoral Society, p. 22.   [2] Ibid., pp. 159f.
[3] Reinhold Niebuhr, The Children of Light and the Children of Darkness (Nisbet, 1945), p. vi.   [4] Ibid., p. vi.

from liberal democracy,[1] while both, as being idealistic, are children of the light in contrast with the children of darkness who are characterised by moral cynicism and exemplified in recent history by Nazi Germany. On the other hand, both liberalism and Marxism, although they are democratic, have this deficiency in common, that if they do not have the malice of cynicism they are thoroughly infected by stupidity. Marxism is as prone as liberalism to assume the shape and character of an oligarchy, and the ultimate cause is that both are much too easily optimistic, and in this connection easy optimism is the very hallmark of stupidity. The fundamental error of our modern age is not, after all, the individualism of liberalism, but the sheer optimism of both liberalism and Marxism. " Perhaps," says Dr. Niebuhr,[2] " the most remarkable proof of the power of this optimistic creed which underlies democratic thought is that Marxism, which is ostensibly a revolt against it, manages to express the same optimism in another form." As between them, it may be that Marxism is to be preferred on account of its realisation of the human need of community, but this advantage is overshadowed by their common deficiency, for, as Professor Niebuhr has it,[3] " Marxism expects men to be as tame and social on the other side of the revolution as Adam Smith and Jeremy Bentham thought them to be tame and prudential on this side of the revolution." " Democracy requires something more than a religious devotion to moral ideals. It requires religious humility."[4] And that means amongst other things an unfailing readiness to submit to examination and criticism our moral and social principles[5] and all our systems of order and justice.

This, of course, brings us very much closer to the authentic Niebuhr of today, who is pre-eminently a theologian, and the process of development is carried a stage

---

[1] Cf. ibid., p. 29.   [2] Ibid., p. 28.   [3] Ibid., p. 46.
[4] Ibid., p. 104.   [5] Cf. Ibid., p. 58.

further in *Faith and History* where he allows that society is capable of a limited but real measure of moral renewal [1] and gives as a significant instance the transformation whereby in " many of the most healthy of modern nations " absolute monarchies, bowing before the storms of opposition, became instead constitutional monarchies, finding that their " powerlessness provided the community with a new form of power, which was completely compatible with the requirements of a more democratic justice." [2]   Dr. Niebuhr has travelled a long way indeed between *Moral Man and Immoral Society* on the one hand and *Faith and History* on the other.   It is as if his political thought and his theology were two separate streams which, each passing under many bridges, finally become one that is both broad and deep.

There remains the question, however, whether this confluence of thought has involved corresponding changes of emphasis in Dr. Niebuhr's religious thinking.   We have already seen that, writing in 1939, just before the delivery of Professor Niebuhr's Gifford Lectures, Principal Baillie was able to describe him as theologically indebted to Karl Barth, and the question is therefore whether Dr. Niebuhr may still fairly be regarded as a Barthian.   There is no doubt of course that he has learned from Dr. Barth, as indeed all contemporary theology which professes to be alive has learned.   The dire events of our troubled twentieth century have conspired with Karl Barth to render outdated and outmoded the liberal theology against which he is essentially in revolt.   It is not only Barth but our western experience of life in these times which has barred the way against any easy return to liberalism in theology.   But theology can learn from Dr. Barth and can at the same time, without evincing any tendency to return to liberalism, make a decisive departure from the essentially Barthian standpoint.   This is so because (*a*) Dr. Barth recognises the transcendent greatness of God, the first

[1] *Cf. Faith and History*, pp. 254ff.   [2] *Ibid.*, p. 257.

importance therefore of the divine initiative and the divine revelation, and the universal corruption wrought in man by sin so that revelation must be thought of as creating its own response ; but (*b*) he recognises these in such an absolute and one-sided fashion that the object of God's love seems to vanish before our eyes.

The decisive point in this connection is the manner in which revelation is conceived as creating its own response ; and it is clear that Dr. Barth pictures it very much after the fashion of a creation out of nothing. According to Dr. Barth, in other words, the object of God's love is little better than empty space ; and it is here that theologians who have considerable sympathy with Dr. Barth find themselves compelled to part company with him.   Of these perhaps Professor Emil Brunner is chief and his main concern is to add some substance to the object of divine grace.   This he does, as we have seen, by recognising as a point of contact what he calls the formal *imago*, not the content in any degree of our humanity, but its bare form, our formal rationality and responsibility.   This, of course, is a step in the right direction, but it is no more than a step.   Indeed, it is so short a step that it leaves Dr. Brunner in a far less stable position than Dr. Barth himself.   All that we have on the human side of the divine-human encounter, as a point of contact for divine grace, is an academic abstraction, not the world which God so loves, but the mere ghost of humanity.

What then has been Dr. Niebuhr's position in relation to this problem ?   This is not an easy question to answer, for Dr. Niebuhr is not always consistent with himself, but the final outcome of the impressive argument in the Gifford Lectures seems to be very much the same as Dr. Brunner's conclusion.   Where the latter speaks of a form which has lost its proper content, Dr. Niebuhr talks of a structure which completely lacks its corresponding perfection ; and, if he does contrive to go somewhat beyond the continental theologian's position, it is largely by the addition of a shadow to Dr. Brunner's ghost of humanity, a shadow, though ghosts have no shadows, in the shape of a thoroughly uneasy, a completely bad conscience—and that seems to be a contradiction in terms. There are, of course, some statements in these Lectures which suggest a more substantial point of contact for God's self-revelation, but on the whole this seems to be the considered opinion which Dr. Niebuhr adopts.   His analysis of the matter, he says,[1]

> leads to the conclusion that sin neither destroys the structure by which man is man, nor yet eliminates the sense of obligation towards the essential nature of man, which is the remnant of his perfection.   This sense of obligation is, in fact, the claim which the essential nature of man makes upon him in his present sinful state.   The virtue which corresponds to the true nature of man therefore appears to sinful man in the form of law.   It is the " good that I would " but which " I do not."   It is " the commandment which was ordained to life " but which " I found to be unto death " (Romans vii), of which St. Paul speaks.   It is unto death because the law states the requirements without helping man to fulfil them.   In fact it heightens sin by arousing sinful egotism to a more conscious defiance of the essential nature of man (Romans vii, 7).

And yet Dr. Niebuhr persistently gives the impression that he intends to do very much more than this, perhaps nowhere more clearly than in his judgment upon the debate between Dr. Barth and Dr. Brunner.

> In this debate [he says],[2] Brunner seems to me to be right and Barth wrong ; but Barth seems to win the debate because Brunner accepts too many of Barth's presuppositions in his fundamental premises to be able to present his own position with plausibility and consistency.   Barth is able to prove Brunner inconsistent, but that does not necessarily prove him to be wrong.

Indeed, it is scarcely too much to say that there is

[1] Reinhold Niebuhr, *Nature and Destiny of Man*, Vol. I (Nisbet, 1941), p. 289.
[2] *Ibid.*, Vol. II (Nisbet, 1943), p. 66 note.

another Niebuhr who lurks behind the scenes in the
Gifford Lectures but comes out more into the open in his
later book, *Faith and History*.   It seems that when Dr.
Niebuhr starts with the central doctrines of the Christian
faith he finds it difficult to escape from Dr. Barth and
not easy to go beyond Dr. Brunner ; but he knows perfectly well that the latter has stopped short of the truth.
On the other hand, when Dr. Niebuhr gives his attention
to questions of Christian morals and practical philosophy
he succeeds in adumbrating a much more defensible
position than either Dr. Barth's or Dr. Brunner's ; and
this is evident from the argument of *Faith and History*.

Here Dr. Niebuhr's intention is to give an account of
the Christian interpretation of history and to distinguish
it from those of classicism and modernism ; and to his
understanding of it there are two main sides, (i) that
history is a process, and that within it there are indefinite
possibilities of progress and fulfilment ; and (ii) that none
the less these historical fulfilments are always provisional,
tentative, and proximate, and that the final fulfilment
of history lies beyond history and is the object of the
eschatological expectation of the Christian faith. There
is both despair and optimism in this outlook, despair of
any final fulfilment within history itself, optimism regarding the indefinite progress that is none the less possible ;
and these are held together because every new progressive achievement is brought under the judgment that,
perversely setting man at its centre, it falls short of the
best that God has designed.   This Christian view of
history obviously represents a very finely balanced perspective, and it is not surprising that time and again the
balance has been lost and Christian thought has fallen
on one side or the other of its true position.   Moreover,
although this Christian view is certainly known only to
faith which involves repentance, it is capable of a limited
rational validation, positive and negative.   It is ration-
ally intelligible, and it makes contact positively and
negatively with what other men believe.   It is, as the

late Principal William Fulton said in a review, " ration-ally relevant." [1]

Now the picture here portrayed represents a consider-able advance upon the earlier account of a structure completely lacking its corresponding virtue and perfec-tion which none the less persists, not indeed as realisa-tion, but as requirement only.   It is much nearer the truth to acknowledge the validity both of the moral insight and of the achievements of ordinary men, and yet to see these coming under the judgment both of God and of the ultimate ideal.   This is not indeed for Dr. Niebuhr an entirely new view for in some ways it is a reiteration of what he said in a much earlier work,[2] and yet there are significant differences to be discovered. In particular, it is clear that while adhering to a pro-found combination of pessimism and optimism Dr. Niebuhr has shed the moral cynicism, especially in rela-tion to collective behaviour, which was so prominent in *Moral Man and Immoral Society*, and found a place too in *An Interpretation of Christian Ethics*.[3]   In its place there is now in *Faith and History* an important admission of the possibility of fulfilment on the collective level as well as the individual ; [4]   there is a commendable recognition of communal virtue ; [5] and there is finally an acknow-ledgment of the virtue that communities may have *by grace*,[6] that is, by the identity of direction obtaining between their imperfect purposes and a higher good than they are ready to serve.

All this marks, if not a significant change of emphasis, a significant development of thought.   But if, in loyalty to the truth as he apprehends it, Dr. Niebuhr has allowed himself to go so far, should he not have allowed himself to go much farther in his Gifford Lectures than he actually did ?   If he allows that the Christian faith is

[1] *The Expository Times*, Vol. LXI, p. 138.
[2] *An Interpretation of Christian Ethics*.
[3] *Cf. op. cit.*, p. 150, p. 189.   [4] *Cf. op. cit.*, pp. 243ff.
[5] *Cf. ibid.*, p. 251.   [6] *Cf. ibid.*, pp. 252ff.

capable even of a limited rational validation should he
not also allow that the Christian revelation makes contact in man with considerably more than an academic
abstraction ?   If he allows in history itself and in ordinary life even tentative and provisional fulfilments, on
the collective as well as the individual level, should he
not regard these as affording a point of contact for that
divine grace through which alone can come the final
fulfilment of all life and history ?   Indeed, has not Dr.
Niebuhr stopped short in the process of integrating his
theological insights on the one hand and his moral and
political insights on the other ?   On the other hand, and
at the same time, has he not been working in the direction of the truth ?   Is it not in fact a major task of contemporary theology to affirm the ethical pessimism of a
profound Christian insight without affirming at the same
time a moral cynicism which has been refuted again and
again ?   For does not the work of grace confirm, condemn and transform in a single act all our virtues and
aspirations, bringing them into captivity to the will of
Christ and centring them not in man but in God ?   But
if in the light of our argument these questions all demand
an affirmative answer it means that the theological position which Dr. Niebuhr seeks to occupy, and to which
he also endeavours to lead his readers, is one which is
both ethical and evangelical.

Not only is this the case, but also, on reflection, it is
apparent at what points, in what contexts and with what
concepts, Dr. Niebuhr comes most closely to this position, and at what points he removes further away.   In
general he approaches most nearly to this position when
he is thinking, not of man in the abstract, but of man
or men in their characteristically human situation, in
their essentially social situation in which they are confronted by other men and, whether they realise it or not,
confronted also by God.   Thus when Dr. Niebuhr makes
the point that " neither the finiteness of the human mind
nor the sinful corruption of the mind nor the ' ideological

taint' in all human culture can completely efface the human capacity for the apprehension of the true wisdom," [1] he illustrates his contention by reference to our knowledge of other selves.

> The other self cannot be understood [he says] [2] until he speaks to us. Only the " word " of the other self, coming out of the depth or height of his self-transcendence can finally disclose the other " I " as subject and not merely as object of our knowledge. Only this communication can give the final clue to the peculiar behaviour of the other. This behaviour always contains contradictory elements which make the real meaning of the behaviour something of a mystery. When the other self finally speaks, the self-disclosure of his words partly clarifies obscurities in his previously observed behaviour and partly negates false conclusions which the self has made by trying to understand the other self in terms of its own characteristic prejudices and passions. The knowledge gained from this self-disclosure of the other self does not stand in complete contradiction to the knowledge gained from the observation of his behaviour. . . . The word of self-disclosure is thus partly a completion of incomplete knowledge, partly a clarification of obscurities and contradictions and partly a correction of falsifications. This is exactly the relation of the self-disclosure of God as received by faith to such other knowledge as man has about the " hidden " God.

In all this when Dr. Niebuhr allows the idea of man's essentially social situation to underlie, regulate and guide his thought, as he does not only in his moral and political thinking but in many parts of his theology as well, he is constrained to follow the lines of what seems to be an ethical evangelical theology or what is consonant with such a theology.

When, on the other hand, he allows himself to think, not of men in their characteristically human situation, but of man in the abstract, he seems to me to fall away from this position ; and perhaps nowhere is this more plainly the case than in his important treatment of the *imago dei*. It is on this doctrine of the *imago* that so much

---

[1] *Nature and Destiny of Man*, Vol. II, pp. 65f.   [2] *Ibid.*, pp. 67f.

theological controversy has centred, and it is in respect
of his treatment of it that Dr. Niebuhr's judgment on
Dr. Brunner seems to apply also to himself, the judgment
that he " accepts too many of Barth's presuppositions in
his fundamental premises to be able to present his own
position with plausibility and consistency." Moreover,
one of these presuppositions, which Dr. Niebuhr sometimes accepts, is that in theology man is to be treated not
in relation to the peculiarly human situation, but in the
abstract, as the bare product of God's creative activity,
the activity of God *as Creator*. Indeed it is not only Dr.
Barth and those who are influenced by him, it is almost
any specific doctrine of the *imago dei* which tends to treat
man in this way ; and yet although the Bible plainly
teaches that man is made in the image of God it does not
teach any specific doctrine of the *imago* and it knows
nothing of man in the abstract, in the way that specific
doctrines of the *imago* pretend to know him. The Bible
knows nothing of man out of his peculiarly human situation ; it knows nothing of him as the bare product of the
creative activity of God. Even the narrative of the
Creation, in which if anywhere we should expect to find
it, is none the less ignorant of any conception of man as
created to exist and not as created to exist in a certain
way, in certain relationships to the rest of the creation,
to his fellow-creatures and to God. In other words, the
narrative of the Creation is ignorant of a creation which
is creation and no more, which is creation devoid of
purpose.

And God said, Let us make man in our image, after our
likeness ; and let them have dominion over the fish of the
sea, and over the fowl of the air, and over the cattle, and
over all the earth, and over every creeping thing that
creepeth upon the earth. So God created man in his own
image, in the image of God created he him ; male and
female created he them. And God blessed them, and God
said unto them, Be fruitful, and multiply, and replenish the
earth, and subdue it ; and have dominion over the fish of

the sea, and over the fowl of the air, and over every living thing that moveth upon the earth. . . .

In all this there is not a single hint of a God who is Creator and not, at the same time, Ruler and Judge as well, nor is there the slightest suggestion of man in the abstract, man out of relationship, man as the bare product of creation, as creature and no more.

In spite of this, Dr. Barth, in the earlier phase of this part of his theology, takes man out of his human situation in which he is confronted by his fellows, even out of his Biblical situation in which he is confronted by God, as Creator, Ruler and Judge, and, under the influence of a non-Biblical, metaphysical preconception of God as predominantly Creator, treats man in the abstract and argues that in him the *imago dei* is abolished and destroyed by sin.   Dr. Brunner follows this example, although, in an endeavour to keep more closely to the facts, he insists on making a further abstraction within the original one, distinguishing between the form and the content of the *imago* as it is conceived as belonging to man in the abstract.   Even in the latest version of Dr. Barth's thought, which seems at first sight to recognise the social quality of man's situation in its emphasis upon the man-woman relationship, the I-Thou relationship, the fact that his moral and social behaviour is made to appear as a natural fact about him, and not as containing ideals and standards to which he is subject, is evidence that man is still being treated in the abstract.   It is because he looks on man in this way that Dr. Barth can speak of these social relationships as if they were *internal* to man, and, accordingly, can find in them an image of God who being three Persons is yet but one God ; and it is thus too, perhaps, that he can reduce the variety of social behaviour to a relationship between male and female. When Dr. Niebuhr also adopts this standpoint he is compelled to follow closely in Barthian footsteps, especially Dr. Brunner's, influenced, I believe, not so much by the preconception of God as predominantly Creator as by its related idea of man in the abstract as the bare product of creativity. Dr. Niebuhr, however, has another point of view, a much more adequate one, from which he sees man fairly and squarely in his human situation and in his Biblical situation, confronted by men and confronted by God, and from which, in consequence, he can and must speak, not of a " part " of man's being which may be " lost " or " destroyed "—these after all are only metaphors which may in theology be dangerously misleading, and for the literal use of which the Bible offers not a shred of justification—but of personal relationships which may suffer distortion and corruption.

In the last resort, therefore, it seems to me that the judgment upon Dr. Niebuhr's theology cannot be precisely the same as his judgment upon Dr. Brunner's ; for in his own case there is an even more fundamental cause of inconsistency—the influence in his theological thinking of two different systems of ideas. Both of these are evangelical, but, while one is ethical, the other is not ; and, in my opinion, it is the ethical which becomes increasingly predominant.

CHAPTER VI

CROSSROADS IN THEOLOGY

Not a few commentators have noted and criticised
in Dr. Barth's exposition of his theology a persistent quality of intransigence and dogmatism
which cannot be completely accounted for as the result
of a thinker's vigorous expression of his own thought.
It is only to be expected that when Dr. Barth takes the
trouble to expound his position he intends us to understand that he believes what he says and that he does not
believe what he denies. And it would be unreasonable
to ask him to accept every criticism that is made against
him. But there is more to it than that. His intransigent dogmatism has another source. It is not merely
that Dr. Barth thinks that his own position is true and
that other positions are false. It is rather that he regards
any departure from his own system as *ipso facto* a departure from evangelical theology and a return to
liberalism. But this is an unjustifiable assumption, as
is evidenced by the trend away from Barthianism by
some of its strongest sympathisers. The truth is that,
so far from coinciding with the entire area of evangelical
theology, Barthianism occupies a quite peculiar position
within its borders. It provides, not *the* evangelical
theology—it is given to no-one to do that—but *an*
evangelical theology with highly distinctive marks of
its own. Like all evangelical theology it is empirical
in the broad sense that it emphasises what is given to
man. The gift of God is eternal life, and eternal life is
the gift of God. It is by grace that we are saved through
faith and that faith not of our own making. In more
general theological terms, Barthianism, like all evangelical theology, lays great stress upon revelation, and
upon revelation, not as an inert object, but as a divine

activity, not only once and for all at a moment in time past, but also now and for all time.

On the other hand, unlike all evangelical theology, Barthian theology, in being thus rightly empirical, pushes to an extreme this insight which it shares with evangelical theology as a whole, and manifests itself within the evangelical realm as a theology which is *radically* empirical. It does this most clearly in the quite radical sense which it imparts to the contention of evangelical theology in general, that revelation not only retains the initiative for God but also creates its characteristic response in man. The response to revelation is also, and absolutely, given. No theological affirmation could be more radically empirical than that ; and in making it Barthianism, wittingly or unwittingly, follows a parallel path to the influential philosophical movement of logical positivism. The intellectual and spiritual conditions of the modern world, which have facilitated the spread of this philosophical faith, and, incidentally, as we have seen, of the political creeds which in Dr. Joad's words are at once the distinction and the disgrace of the present age, have also prepared the way for the Barthian theology.

Even so, however, such observations cannot fairly pose as a final assessment of Barthianism, for although Barthian theology is indeed in its own way a radically empirical theology, its radical empiricism displays significant differences in comparison with the cruder empiricism of the philosophical school. And, although the radical empiricism of Barthianism doubtless helps to explain its external success as a theology (but not its success as a religious movement of great consequence), it does not provide the ultimate clue to its interior logic. For this the student must look elsewhere, to the realisation that God is subject, an insight which stems from the work of Soren Kierkegaard, Ferdinand Ebner and Martin Buber, and which is more compatible with existentialist thinking than with that of logical positivism.

But here, too, the radical character of Barthianism is evident, for it is so emphasised that God is subject that it is forgotten that man in his derivative way is also subject. For the most part, this is forgotten rather than denied. Indeed it is sometimes clearly affirmed by Barthians that man is subject, but the affirmation is immediately surrounded by more fundamental contentions which ultimately deny it, in particular by the quite fundamental contention that through and through God is to man as Creator is to creature and that every other relationship is a modification of that one, or, as it were, falls within it. And yet, manifestly, unless man is created as something more than mere creature, as something more than the bare product of creative activity, unless, indeed, he is created as a relatively independent subject, no significant relationships, certainly no ethical relationships, are possible. If man is simply the product of divine power—if, in other words, man is mere creature through and through, a being whose metaphysical, as well as moral, essence is to be defined exhaustively in terms of his dependence upon God his Creator—then even the distorted relationship of sin is for him an impossibility. Such a being could not sin. But if, in spite of this, sin is posited, there is nothing left in man relevant to the re-establishment of a right relationship to God, or rather there is nothing left in man (sinful man is, strictly speaking, nothing at all), and the right relationship, if it comes, is absolutely and completely another, a new, creation. It was to avoid such conclusions as these and to give substance and reality to the object of God's love manifested in the Gospel that Dr. Brunner diverged from Dr. Barth in the first instance, holding that, although the content of the *imago dei* in which man was created was utterly destroyed by sin, the form was preserved intact. But, as we have already seen in effect, the meagre result of this distinction was simply to substitute an academic abstraction for a nonentity, while all the time the initial assumption that mere creatureliness constituted the inner essence of humanity was not called in question. The all-pervading assumption remained that God is first and last our Creator and that the finally constitutive fact of man's being is not anything he is, not anything that God has made him, but the relationship of dependence in which he stands to God, just as by definition a mathematical point has position but no magnitude. In comparison with this common ground, Dr. Brunner's divergence appears somewhat minute, and yet it was the occasion of a vigorous, and sometimes heated, controversy between himself and Dr. Barth, in which the former was handicapped by the considerable extent of his continuing agreement with his theological adversary.

More recently, as a result of the almost drastic alterations which Dr. Barth has introduced into his teaching in the second part of the third volume of his *Dogmatik*, published in 1948, that vigorous controversy has been replaced by a rather precarious alliance. So great do these changes appear to Dr. Brunner that he has been driven to exclaim, " Is it Karl Barth who wrote these things ? Indeed it is ! Not however the Barth of 1934, but of 1948—the new Barth." [1] Nor can it be denied that the changes are important. Dr. Barth has certainly made significant amendments to his teaching. But—and it is this that is of consequence in the present connection—how little is really changed underneath, as a ship may turn, now to the south, now to the north, and remain all the time anchored in the same place !

What then are these changes ? Their main effect is that it is no longer taught that the image of God is destroyed by sin. On the contrary, it is now affirmed, the image survives ; and it consists of two parts or strands, man's relationship to God and man's relationship to man, or, as Dr. Barth prefers (giving unusual weight to the Biblical statement that man was created

---

[1] Emil Brunner, " The New Barth," *Scottish Journal of Theology*, June, 1951, p. 124.

male and female), man's relationship to woman. Even natural sinful man displays or possesses the image of God in which he is made in these two directions. So far as the second strand is concerned, Dr. Barth has ungrudgingly re-instated natural morality in the form of natural love and helpfulness, but he has re-instated it, as I have already said, not as providing a norm or ideal, but as a natural fact—it is not that natural man ought to behave thus, but much rather that he does. The first strand of the image consists in man's election in Christ which human sin can neither affect nor annul, and indeed, not only in man's election in Christ, but in his faithful and obedient response to that election, which Dr. Barth finds it difficult to distinguish and dissociate from it. But is this the sinful natural man of whom Dr. Barth is speaking ? The answer to this question remains at the end of Dr. Barth's discussion the subject of considerable doubt, and this in spite of the fact that so long as that doubt remains the implication is that either only Christians are men or all men are Christians.

On the other hand, whatever answer be given to these questions in the development of Dr. Barth's thought, it is clear that already he has made an important revision of his earlier teaching, which in some ways at least brings it nearer to the truth and even raises the question whether Dr. Barth himself is still a Barthian. One account of the inner meaning of the change has been suggested by Dr. Brunner.

> Is not this [he asks][1] what has happened between 1934 and 1948, that then Barth in his preoccupation with saving grace ignored the grace of creation, whilst now he seems to be inclined to identify saving grace and the grace of creation, to let the former be merged in the latter ?

The trouble with this verdict is, however, that Dr. Barth seems as guilty of this merging of saving grace into the grace of creation in his earlier phase as in his later—this

[1] " The New Barth," *Scottish Journal of Theology*, June, 1951, pp. 128f.

was indeed a main burden of the complaint against him [1]
—and that he would have been less guilty of it in his post-
war thought if, but only if, he had been able to represent
man's positive relationship to man as a norm and God's
election of him in Christ as a claim, and not, in both
cases, simply and solely as a fact, whether of nature or
of grace. It is because they are represented fundamentally as fact that Dr. Barth's account of the *imago*
in both its strands is equivocal and inconclusive, swing-
ing indeterminately between the full reality of the fact
and its total absence, for either a fact is, or it is not a
fact ; and they are represented fundamentally as fact
because Dr. Barth remains a Barthian and, accordingly,
still assimilates saving grace to a preconceived " grace "
of creation.

What has happened between 1934 and 1948 is not
that he has begun to make this assimilation, but that,
having made it from the beginning of this period, he has
been driven in the meantime to give a different, a more
positive account of natural man.   Previously, the effect
of sin was a total effect, was barely distinguishable from
non-existence, the object of God's love was virtually
reduced to nothing.   Now, it is restored to reality, but
in turn it has become barely distinguishable from
redeemed and rescued humanity, from Christian humanity, and, most significantly, as indeed one might have
expected, the reality of sin is called in question, it is
described as an " ontological impossibility." [2]   Within
the assimilation of saving grace to creative activity there
are two main possibilities : Either sin and no positive
content for fallen humanity, or else a positive content and
no sin.   Dr. Barth tends to favour the one alternative
whereas at one time he was all for the other.   Where
grace and creation are insufficiently distinguished either

---

[1] *Cf.* J. Baillie, *Our Knowledge of God* (Oxford University Press, 1939),
pp. 17–27, especially pp. 24ff., where Barth is accused of " obliterating the
important theological distinction between the creative and the gracious
activity of God."

[2] *Dogmatik*, Vol. III, 2, p. 162 ; *cf.* p. 235.

sin is nothing or sinful man is nothing. And, the more the former possibility is followed, the less evangelical, and at the same time the more metaphysical, does a theology become.

Although there are the two main possibilities within the assimilation of saving grace to creative activity, Dr. Brunner has himself tried to work out a third, by means of the unreal abstraction of form from content and content from form ; and yet it is perhaps Dr. Brunner who reveals most clearly the defining presupposition of Barthian theology. He does so when he insists that in being confronted by Christ we are made aware of our creatureliness,[1] that the heart of creatureliness is responsibility,[2] and that responsibility is a relation, not a substance.[3] It is difficult, indeed impossible, to express this point of view without positing an element of substance and endowment, something distinguishable, though not necessarily separable, from the relationship to God. Dr. Brunner posits it again and again—the very word " responsibility " (in his sense, " ability to respond ") posits it—but inasmuch as he does so he contradicts his fundamental insight, at least the insight which is surpassed in fundamental character only by the evangelical dependence on revelation. " Christian Faith makes responsibility the heart of human personal existence,"[4] he tells us, but of course he gives to responsibility his own meaning, which I have already argued to be a derivative meaning, that of answerability. In so doing he is led to put the cart before the horse by his preconception regarding the centrality of creatureliness. On the other hand, the fully moral concept of responsibility, which Dr. Brunner describes as legal responsibility, is set aside as the product of sin. " Legal responsibility is . . . already a result of the false autonomy of man, and has a correlative relation to it."[5]

[1] Emil Brunner, *The Christian Doctrine of Creation and Redemption* (Lutterworth Press, 1952), pp. 54–55. [2] *Ibid.*, pp. 56–57. [3] *Ibid.*, pp. 59f.
[4] *Ibid.*, p. 87. [5] *Ibid.*, p. 61 ; *cf.* pp. 119ff.

This is the decisive and fateful parting of the ways within the field of contemporary evangelical theology. On the one side the concept of creatureliness and the cognate concept of answerability are taken as regulative ; on the other, the moral ideas of divine sovereignty and strict moral responsibility are acknowledged as fundamental. It is not difficult to see on which side of the line of division Barthian theology takes its stand, or to realise that in its later variations it has not changed sides. " All the differences within created existence," says Dr. Brunner,[1] " living and dead, free and un-free, human and non-human, are insignificant, in comparison with the uncreated Being of God and created being, between God and the world." And that remarkably frank and clear statement puts the matter in a nutshell. It is here, while all the time learning from Dr. Barth's outstanding contribution to theology, that the theologian must finally say " yes " or " no " to Barthianism. The road on which the religious thinker travels in his search for theological truth divides at other points. There is a parting of the ways between the Roman Catholic account of Christian faith and the Protestant one, and a parting of the ways between liberalism and evangelical theology ; but besides these there is another, within the evangelical field, according as the ruling idea by which the revelation is theologically interpreted is found in the divine creativity or in the divine sovereignty and grace.

Needless to say, on neither side is it denied that men are the creatures of God's hand and that it is He alone who preserves them in existence. Accordingly, it must be admitted that in a real sense men are ontologically or metaphysically dependent upon God ; but alongside that acknowledgment ethical evangelical theology sees that within this metaphysical dependence, that is to say, under God, there is a real metaphysical independence which is the indispensable basis of the moral

[1] *Ibid.*, p. 21.

dependence, the trust, love and faith, to which men are called in God's mercy, and for which they are claimed by His grace. To deny this relative metaphysical independence, to say that man is completely, in every moment of his existence and in the very centre of his being, a mere creature, to dissolve the " what " of humanity into a relation in which it stands to God, to imply that man is something that God does and not something that He makes, are to render moral dependence, sin, grace and faith all equally ontological impossibilities. And yet this is what Barthian theology does, and, in doing it, professes to find its justification in the Christian revelation. In this matter, says Dr. Brunner,[1] " we must start from the Centre," that is from Christ, and " to be aware of the holy Loving God, and to be aware of the fact that my nature is created by God, comes to the same thing."

This, of course, is not all. Alongside this governing train of thought, permeating it and largely obscuring it, there is another of equal, if not greater, importance in which the Barthian theologian speaks with the accents of a genuinely evangelical theology of such topics as universal sin and sovereign grace, and this in spite of the fact that the other trend of thought leaves no logical room for these. On the contrary, these characteristic topics of evangelical thought demand an ethical theology, one which finds in Christ first a Saviour and a Sovereign, and only then the Word that was in the beginning by whom all things were made, and not vice versa. In other words, they demand an ethical theology for which the absolute moral authority and sovereignty of Christ are, in the order of human knowledge, in the order of faith, prior, not posterior, to the conviction that He is one with God the Creator. And yet in Barthianism, in spite of their incongruity, the metaphysical and evangelical strains are almost inextricably intermingled, so that the thoroughly evangelical intention of Dr. Barth

[1] *The Christian Doctrine of Creation and Redemption*, p. 55.

and those who think with him cannot seriously be called in question. Thus it happens that the peculiar metaphysical quality of Barthianism is not easily detected. Barthian language is the language of evangelical theology, and it is only here and there at decisive points that the Barthian's twofold loyalty becomes evident, a loyalty to revelation and a loyalty, hardly less, to a certain metaphysical preconception concerning creatureliness.

Perhaps no stronger or more impressive evidence of this could be found than in a comparison of Barthian theology with that of P. T. Forsyth, in whose work the continental movement has aroused a quickened interest and who has been widely hailed as offering, at least in some degree, an important anticipation of Dr. Barth. According to Forsyth the fact of sin, " world sin, sin in dominion, sin solidary if not hereditary, yea, sin which integrates us into a Satanic kingdom," [1] is the predominant factor in every human situation and in ours ; and consequently, he holds, history must be viewed " under the category of judgment . . . and not under that of progress. Eschatology goes much deeper than evolution." [2] Here, evidently, is another vigorous critic of liberal theology like Dr. Barth himself ; and yet, we think, the final outcome of any adequate comparison of the two thinkers must be that alongside the fundamental agreement of their respective theologies there is an almost equally fundamental divergence and that Forsyth's work is as much a corrective to, as an anticipation of, Barthianism.

Dr. Barth's theology, it will be agreed, is essentially a protest against theological liberalism or rationalism, that movement which found its centre of gravity in the reason and moral consciousness of natural men, and which frequently justified this approach by insisting that human reason, both theoretical and practical, is the divine element in our humanity, in other words, by emphasising the immanence of God. On this view the

[1] *The Justification of God*, p. 31.   [2] *Ibid.*, p. 178.

chief end of man, however it may be expressed, is to
follow reason and conscience wherever they may lead, to
follow them into their highest reaches of vision and
attainment, and to come at last along this road to the
kingdom of God ; and, on the same view, Jesus becomes
that one in whom the divine in man rose pre-eminently
to the surface.   At every point, whether confronted by
daily duty or final destiny, we are dealing, not in any
sense, with two worlds, but with one world which has
its centre of gravity in man.   Now it was against all
such thoughts that Dr. Barth very firmly set his face.
He insisted, not on the immanence of God, but on His
transcendence.   God is wholly other, and He is neither
a man nor an extension of our humanity.   Indeed, the
transcendence of God is the fundamental keynote of Dr.
Barth's entire theology ; and from this central emphasis
there follows closely another, an insight of equal importance, that if we are to know God it can only be by His
self-revelation.   We cannot discover Him by ourselves.
It is only by His grace and at His pleasure that we can
come to see Him at all.   Reasoned argument, philosophy,
metaphysics, natural theology, these can take us no part
of the way.   We can only go this way to God if God first
comes to us, if He reveals Himself, as in fact He has done
in Jesus Christ His Son.   Jesus, therefore, is not a man
as we are, not *merely* a man in whom our common
divinity has come pre-eminently to the surface and has
taken control.   He is essentially the Word of God, the
One in whom God reveals Himself to us and declares
Himself to all His children.   His birth is not merely
like ours, it is the incarnation ; His death is not merely
ours, it is the atonement.   Moreover, since God is
wholly other and we can only know Him by His own
gracious self-revelation, we cannot hope to know Him
as we know the objects in the world around us and as
perhaps we may come to know our human nature ;
that is to say, we cannot hope to know God by clear
and distinct ideas producing a knowledge marked by

transparency and coherence. Rather, in this direction, we shall see through a glass darkly, and there will be many paradoxes and much mystery in our understanding.

These are of course characteristically Barthian positions, and yet, although some of his work was published before the first World War, P. T. Forsyth does provide an impressive anticipation of them. Equally with Dr. Barth he has a quarrel with rationalism. The crucial question within Christianity, he tells us, is this,

> Is saving faith a Rationalism, *i.e.* a faith in universal ideas, intuitions, or processes, which have no exclusive relation to a fixed point in history? Or is it gathered to such a point, in the historic Christ, where God, in presence, actually offers himself *to* man in judgment and for man in Grace? [1]

" Are we to demand that Christ shall submit to the standard of certain principles or ideals which we bring to him from our human nature at its heart's highest and its thought's best? Or as our new creator is he his own standard . . . ? " [2] The final issue, he tells us, " is between a rational Christianity and a redemptive." [3] Again, he says, the great question within the Church is between theological liberalism and " a free but positive theology, which is essentially evangelical." [4] Moreover, the great fault of rationalism or theological liberalism, which Forsyth also describes as ego-centric and anthropocentric, is that in it " God is drawn into the circle of our spiritual interests, the interests of man's spiritual culture, as its mightiest ally and helper." [5] It is assumed that " God were no God if He cared for anything more than He did for His creatures " ; [6] and the anthropocentric religion which results is marked by " man's preoccupation with humanity and its spiritual civilisation and culture." [7] Further, as Forsyth tells [8]

---

[1] *The Person and Place of Jesus Christ*, p. 95.
[2] *Ibid.*, p. 95.   [3] *Ibid.*, p. 96.   [4] *Ibid.*, p. 84.
[5] *Ibid.*, p. 28.   [6] *The Justification of God*, p. 11.
[7] *Ibid.*, p. 24.   [8] *Cf. ibid.*, pp. 70ff.

us, the difference between this outlook and its alternative
in evangelical theology is that for the former God is
immanent, for the latter transcendent. Our present-day
Protestantism rises from the union or intermingling of
two distinct streams, and because they are distinct their
coming together produces confusion. The one is the
Reformation and the other is the Illumination.

> For the one the great matter was God's transcendence over
> the world, for the other it was His immanence in it. So the
> one degenerated to Deism, the other to Pantheism. . . .
> For the one Christ is absolute, for the other He is but relative
> to the history from which He arose.[1]

Between them a choice must be made, and, says Forsyth quite clearly and distinctly, " we take the Reformation side of our Protestantism for a stand, and not the
Illuminationist." [2] Thus Forsyth did take his stand in
a position later to be occupied by Dr. Karl Barth.
Moreover, in taking his stand here, Forsyth put God's
revelation of Himself in Christ at the very centre of his
thought and theology. " In the whole region of revelation," he says [3] of Jesus, " he carries himself in a
sovereign and final way." The power of Jesus did not
lie in any novel truth that he propounded about man or
God, but " in the new divine personality, and the
redeeming, consummating act of God effected in it." [4]
The choice between a doctrine of transcendence and one
of immanence is, as we have seen, a choice between a
rational theology and a redemptive, and that is now
seen to involve a choice between reason and revelation.
But revelation must not be rationalised. It is a mistaken treatment of revelation which sees it " as something propositional rather than redemptive," [5] and the
true idea of revelation is " destroyed by being viewed
as the conveyance of truth about God and His action,

[1] *The Person and Place of Jesus Christ*, p. 189.
[2] *Ibid.*, p. 192.   [3] *Ibid.*, p. 109.
[4] *Ibid.*, p. 64.   [5] *The Justification of God*, p. 84.

instead of God's actual coming and acting." [1]   The
truth is that there is a point in history, " in Christ there
is a spot where we are known far more than we know.
. . . In Christ God is not preached but present. . . .
He does more than justify faith, He creates it." [2]   But
if God reveals Himself in Christ, creating faith, out of
which arises dogma, we must not think that here all
things have been made plain.   " No dogma is adequate
to spiritual reality." [3]   " We are known far more than
we know."   " The greatest of realities is the greatest of
paradoxes," [4] and we cannot hope to escape from that
general situation.

Such are the main points of Forsyth's teaching, and it
is worthwhile considering them at this length for thereby
we can see how very closely they approximate to the
characteristic tenets of Barthianism.   Quite evidently
Forsyth has anticipated Dr. Barth in a remarkable and
impressive manner.   In the one as in the other, God is
regarded as transcendent, revelation is put at the very
centre of theology, reason working in the realm of faith
is allowed only a modest competence, and the way of
rationalism is firmly eschewed.   But if the similarities
between these two theologians are great, the differences
are no less noteworthy, and the careful reader of both
must be arrested by the changed " atmosphere " which
he encounters when he turns from the Swiss thinker to
the British.   If he tries to trace this difference to its
source, he will find that it arises from a difference in
attitude both to reason and, especially, to morality.

Forsyth comes second to none, not even to Dr. Barth,
in his opposition to rationalism, the movement which, in
theology, regards man's reason as divine and capable of
scaling the highest heights of reality, nor could any
thinker place a greater stress upon God's self-revelation
as the indispensable condition of human knowledge of
God.   But it is one thing to oppose rationalism and

[1] *The Justification of God*, p. 84.   [2] *Ibid.*, p. 47.
[3] *The Person and Place of Jesus Christ*, p. 69.   [4] *Ibid.*, p. 70.

quite another to deny reason, and, while Forsyth always takes the former course, he never follows the latter. Reason is involved in the response to revelation which is called faith, and, although it sees only through a glass darkly and has frequently to be content with paradoxical beliefs, the effort to adjust these " could only cease with the paralysis of thought." [1]

When we turn, however, to Dr. Barth it is very far from clear that he likewise does not deny reason in opposing rationalism. For one thing, in his earlier discussions of the *imago dei* in man and the effect upon it of human sin he insists on a doctrine of total corruption. There is in man no point of contact left for the divine revelation, and he argues in the strongest and most emphatic terms that the Christian man is a new creature who owes nothing to the natural man whose place he has taken. Everything natural is irrelevant to faith, and Dr. Barth very decisively turns his back upon it all. Moreover, in outlining the content of Christian faith, as is well known, Dr. Barth gave a very prominent place to the element of paradox, so much so indeed that his theology was known for a time as the dialectical theology ; and in doing this he not only laid greater stress upon the paradoxical character of faith than Forsyth ever did but he tended to treat his paradoxes, not as accidents, vicissitudes, failures on the part of human reason working in the realm of faith and revelation, but as fixed limits to its activity. Thus Professor Niebuhr, who has in some ways come close to Barthianism, has suggested that a paradox may " be accepted as a rational understanding of the limits of rationality." [2] In his later work Dr. Barth has admittedly set aside the existentialism which coloured so much of his earlier thought. Although he might therefore be held, and is indeed sometimes held, to have abandoned his dialectical theology, this does not seem to have happened. Even in

[1] *The Person and Place of Jesus Christ*, p. 72.
[2] *The Nature and Destiny of Man*, Vol. I, p. 278.

the revised edition of his *Prolegomena to Church Dogmatics* he tells us that " the Word of God alone fulfils the concept of paradox with complete strictness, whereas in all other thinkable ' paradoxes ' the opposition between communication and form is such that it can be dissolved from some superior point of vantage." [1] Certainly, in his later writings, he speaks more freely of reason as involved in faith. " Christendom," he now says,[2] " and the theological world were always ill-advised in thinking it their duty for some reason or other, either of enthusiasm or of theological conception, to betake themselves to the camp of an opposition to reason." " Christian faith is . . . rational in the proper sense." [3] Such admissions do suggest that some change has taken place in Dr. Barth's own view of the place of reason in Christian faith. In his latest work room is found for reason, but it is reason illuminated by revelation, or, more specifically, and, one must add, more characteristically, reason completely determined by revelation. " Knowledge of God is a knowledge completely effected and determined from the side of its object, from the side of God." [4] Now this is a considerable concession, whether it can be made consistently or not. But it is still questionable whether, in insisting that this knowledge of God, that reason in this direction, is utterly and completely determined and effected from the side of its object, Dr. Barth has not taken away with his left hand what he has given with his right. Here, if deliberate and emphatic language is to be trusted, reason is purely passive. It is not an activity at all but from first to last a receptivity. But if that is so, it cannot be *illuminated* (as Dr. Barth suggests in one sentence), it can only be *determined* (as he holds in another), and that wholly and completely. In other words, it is not reason at all, it is the name but not the

---

[1] *The Doctrine of the Word of God*, p. 189.

[2] *Dogmatics in Outline*, p. 22. This book was first published in German in 1947 under the title *Dogmatik im Grundriss*.

[3] *Dogmatics in Outline*, p. 23. [4] *Ibid.*, p. 24.

reality. On this point, surely, it is Forsyth who is nearer the truth. Reason *by itself* is incompetent in this field, but with revelation it is illuminated, it is quickened, and it is not immobilised and virtually destroyed. No doubt Dr. Barth is afraid that to allow reason any activity whatsoever is to open the door to human error and disloyalty ; but, on the other hand, to deny the activity of reason is to close the door upon the very possibility of loyalty, truth and obedience.

It is, however, when we consider their respective treatments of morality that the difference between Forsyth and Dr. Barth is most clear. As he was in opposition to rationalism so Dr. Barth is to be found in opposition to moralism. Faith is not morality, nor any smooth extension of morality, as liberalism was prone to suppose. Dr. Barth, in consequence, dismissed morality as an arbitrary factor in human life on a level with chance, and, although in his later work, he has apparently re-instated it in the relationship of man to woman, it is the content without the form which he has provided, morality as a natural fact and not a claim upon the human person, morality in chains and impotent, the semblance not the reality of the moral life. Once again, however, Dr. Barth seems to have failed to distinguish between hostility to the undue magnification of a thing and hostility to the thing itself. And yet such a distinction is clearly demanded by the facts. The alternative to tyranny and dictatorship is not anarchy. Likewise the alternative to moralism in theology is anti-moralism with a hyphen and not antimoralism without it.

Forsyth, on the other hand, never seems to make the mistake of confusing these two very different things. Nothing could be clearer than the moral intention which pervades his whole treatment of evangelical theology. His book on *The Person and Place of Jesus Christ* is appropriately prefaced by a quotation from Bishop Butler to the effect that " morality is the nature of things," and by that is meant a description or indication, not of

morality's content and criterion, but of its status.   " The
study of theology," he says in that book,[1] " must go on
and go forward."   " Dogma is the science of faith," but
that " means the science of religion when religion rises
to the positive faith we have in Christianity, the science
of religion as a moral relation, a living and historic
relation between two personalities, two consciences ;
which in Christianity is a redeeming relation." [2]   What
is needed is the moralising of dogma.   " Yet let it not
be thought that the moralising of dogma makes it less
urgent, less incumbent, less dogmatic.   For what is so
insistent, inevitable, and dogmatic as the categorical
imperative which is at the moral centre ? " [3]   Such a
theology " starts from the conviction that for life and
history the moral is the real, and that the movements of
the Great Reality must be morally construed as they are
morally revealed." [4]   To this fundamentally moral conception of theology Forsyth contrives to remain faithful
in its detailed elaboration.   The plight of natural man
is a moral plight.   His is a " dull ethic which takes no
measure of either his race's sin or a holy God." [5]   He
" does not face the moral problem between the guilty
soul and God " ; [6] and he does not because, as natural
man without revelation, he cannot.   Speaking of the
apostles, Forsyth says that the revelation in Christ
" reorganised their conceptual world by giving it a new
vital centre, and therefore a new reading.   They saw
a new world because a new king was on its throne." [7]
Even the religion of natural humanity is concerned with
man and his weal instead of God and His glory ; but the
self-revelation in Christ as witnessed in the Gospels
and interpreted by the apostles alters this whole situation, and re-establishes it round a new centre, not
man but God.   " In Christ God is not preached but

---

[1] *The Person and Place of Jesus Christ*, p. 213.
[2] *Ibid.*, p. 216.   [3] *Ibid.*, p. 218.
[4] *Ibid.*, pp. 222f.   [5] *Ibid.*, p. 91.
[6] *Ibid.*, p. 24.   [7] *Ibid.*, p. 161.

present. . . . He does more than justify faith, He creates it. . . . We believe because He makes us believe—with a moral compulsion." [1]

It is not to our present purpose to attempt a precise assessment of the adequacy of Forsyth's detailed treatment of his theological themes but to indicate and evaluate his general approach, and, in particular, to contrast it with that of Barthianism as affording an alternative to the latter within the strictly evangelical field ; and to that end it should perhaps be made clear at once that this alternative which Forsyth offers to Barthianism is not by any means a simple return to Ritschlianism. It may be a mistake, as some have suggested, to press the Ritschlian distinction between theoretical judgments and judgments of value so far that it implies that what is valued is unreal ; but, on the other hand, it was misguided and misleading on Ritschl's part to draw such a strict distinction between these two types of judgment in the religious sphere. Forsyth, however, did not commit this error. His quotation from Butler already mentioned makes that clear from the start, and he admits frankly that, when faith reflects upon itself and the revelation to which it is a response, " some metaphysic is involved . . . but it is a metaphysic of the conscience." [2] The great failure of the Ritschlian system, however, was its inability to measure up to the full truth of an evangelical theology. Its tendency was to bring the revelation in Christ within the narrow compass afforded by the ordinary moral consciousness. But if the mark of a truly evangelical theology is the seriousness with which it treats of this revelation, Forsyth's theology, as well as Dr. Barth's, distinguishes itself decisively from Ritschl's. On the other hand, Forsyth's position is differentiated from Dr. Barth's by the fact that its treatment of the revelation is thoroughly ethical, or, at any rate, tries incessantly to be so, whereas Dr. Barth falls

---

[1] *The Justification of God*, p. 47.
[2] *The Person and Place of Jesus Christ*, p. 222.

below this level, not only in his predominantly negative
attitude to morality, but also in his conception of human
reason in faith as being completely determined by its
object and, in consequence, as being perfectly passive.
Over against Ritschl, Forsyth and Dr. Barth both provide a thoroughly evangelical theology; while over
against Dr. Barth, Ritschl and Forsyth alike present what
is intended to be a completely ethical theology.   Ritschl's
failure was an evangelical failure ; Dr. Barth's is an
ethical one ; while Forsyth's constant endeavour was
to outline a theology which would be as ethical as it was
evangelical, and as evangelical as it was ethical.

To such an argument Dr. Barth might well reply by
pointing again to the revelation and by quoting his own
words on an earlier occasion, " How can chance or
morality or any other arbitrary factor set up its own
special law here ? " [1]   But, while that retort may be
decisive with respect to Ritschl (and, even in his case,
subject only to the qualification that our ordinary moral
consciousness, though it has an arbitrary element, is by
no means entirely arbitrary) it misses Forsyth completely.   With him morality does *not* set up its own
special law over the revelation.   Dr. Barth's criticism
holds against theological moralism but not against
ethical theology.   In Forsyth's system morality is not
closed but open.   It does not set up a law but offers at
most a guiding, interpretative, but, above all, *illuminable*
principle.   It does not detract from revelation but provides the means for its exaltation.   Moreover, Dr.
Barth has his own interpretative principle, an inferior
one, not moral but metaphysical, as is evidenced by his
idea of the complete determination of reason in faith
and by his final reduction of positive morality to a
natural fact which does not even prepare the way for the
revelation in Christ.   In spite of his own best intention,
he has not allowed himself to be guided from first to last
by the revelation itself.   Rather, his theological account

[1] *The Knowledge of God and the Service of God,* p. 143.

of Christian faith has been predetermined by a certain idea of transcendence, by a preconception as to how a transcendent God would deal with His creatures, by the notion of man as a mere creature, as one of whom it must be said that the " what " of his being created by God can be identified without remainder with the " that ". Dr. Barth has not been true to the moral realities of the situation. That, he might say, is a merit, since he has succeeded in expelling morality as an active principle from the precincts of faith where, admittedly, it was for a time too much at home. But, if so, he has also unwittingly introduced an arbitrary, amoral and metaphysical element at the very centre of Christian faith.

If this analysis is correct, Dr. Barth can fairly claim to have given to the modern world a thoroughly evangelical theology, but it is not true that any departure from it is of necessity a surrender of the evangelical principle. On the contrary, there is an ethical evangelical theology, distinct from Barthianism but no less evangelical. Indeed, an evangelical theology which is not ethical is evangelical formally but not materially, for the revelation itself is ethical from first to last, and such a theology may even be in danger of ceasing to be evangelical at all.

PART THREE

THEOLOGY AND THE MODERN MIND

CHAPTER VII

THEOLOGY AND FAITH

WHAT is theology ? How is it to be defined ? With what is it concerned ? And why is it pursued ? According to the dictionary, it is the science which treats of God and of man's duty towards Him ; but, while such a definition may have been quite consonant with the medieval conception of the theological task, it does not harmonise with more recent practice in this field. Medieval theology did treat of God, of His existence and of His attributes, and it tended to assimilate positive theology, theology taking its stand upon revelation, to the model and example of natural theology. The transition from natural to positive theology, although it was definitely a transition, was a transition within what was fundamentally the one domain and the one description dealing with that domain. Theology was indeed the science which treats of God and of man's duty towards Him.

To the very conception, however, of such a study the modern mind, and especially the modern religious consciousness, is hostile. God is not an object to be examined and investigated by man, to be analysed into His several attributes and, as it were, put under the microscope as a botanist might proceed to study some rare plant. Nor is it only the peculiar methods of empirical science and the means it employs towards the fulfilment of its acknowledged end that are inappropriate ; it is also the design and purpose of science which is improper when transferred from the objects of the created world to God the Creator of all. God is not an object ; and yet medieval theology, in assimilating positive theology to natural theology, was also assimilating theology as a whole to secular knowledge.

God, on this view, was one object amongst many which the mind of man might attempt to study ; and it is this implication which seems so offensive to the modern religious mind, although it commended itself to no less a figure than Cardinal Newman. " What I mean by Theology is," he said,[1] " . . . simply the Science of God, or the truths we know about God put into system ; just as we have a science of the stars and call it astronomy, or of the crust of the earth and call it geology." Put thus bluntly, however, this idea of theology sets itself quite apart from the predominant contemporary understanding of theological thought, of its competence and its scope. Even Newman felt constrained to define theology as Science with a capital letter and so to make a rather futile concession to the divinity of God ; but modern thought, on the whole, prefers another way, insisting that God is not an object at all.

If then God is no object, how do we come to know Him ? Only by His revelation of Himself to us, by His disclosure of His own person, that is to say, in and out of the fact that God Himself confronts and encounters us, and, so far as the Christian knowledge of God is concerned, in and out of the fact that He encounters us in Jesus Christ His Son. This means, however, that Christian theology, no matter how it is properly to be defined and its purpose described, falls within the area covered and delimited by this relationship in which the grace of God present in Jesus Christ creates faith in man, and in which man's faith answers God's grace. Moreover, this in turn means that Christian theology is not a specification of a more general theology, as zoology and botany might be considered to be each a specification of biology—unless indeed it should appear that God has revealed Himself in other ways in other religious faiths—and it certainly means that natural theology, in so far as it stands altogether apart from

[1] Newman, *Idea of a University*, Vol. II, 7, quoted by J. Baillie, *The Interpretation of Religion* (T. & T. Clark, 1929), p. 6, note.

revelation, is not theology in the same sense as Christian theology. The latter belongs essentially to the sphere of grace and faith, and outside that sphere it does not exist.

Now if this is indeed, as it seems to be, the pre-eminently characteristic insight of modern theology, it is outstandingly due to the work of one theologian, Friedrich Schleiermacher.

> To Schleiermacher [as another theologian has put it] belongs the distinguished merit of having been the first to provide any fully reasoned alternative to rationalism. And the alternative he suggested was one which proved, in not a few important respects, to point in the right direction. Schleiermacher saw clearly that religion must once and for all be made independent of that " effort to penetrate into the nature and substance of things " which found its culmination in modern scientific cosmology.[1]

Moreover, the alternative provided by Schleiermacher is one which restricts the activity of theology to the realm of faith. " We must begin with a conception of the Christian Church, in order to define in accordance therewith what Dogmatics should be and should do, within the Church." [2] In other words, genuine Christian theology can take place only within the Christian Church, or within the area of Christian faith, and can be defined only in relation to that area ; and, although much of Schleiermacher's thought has in the course of time become suspect, and although in particular it has been the target for vigorous if not vehement attacks from a Barthian standpoint, it remains true that this initial and fundamental insight cannot be assailed, and that without it Barthianism itself would not have been possible.

Christian theology, then, falls within, and is to be

---

[1] Baillie, *The Interpretation of Religion*, p. 208, quoting F. Schleiermacher, *Reden*, trans. J. Oman, p. 49.

[2] Schleiermacher, *The Christian Faith* (T. & T. Clark, 1928), p. 3.

defined in relation to, the area of the Christian Church
or the Christian faith, and this procedure obviously presupposes that that area presents itself as a quite distinct
phenomenon which, in turn, can be defined or sufficiently
described so that its identity may be recognised.   Moreover, it is precisely here that divergences begin to occur
in the main stream of characteristically modern theology.
Thus Schleiermacher himself found the essential mark
of religion in the feeling of absolute dependence.   It was
this that constituted faith or piety ; and the Christian
faith is distinguished from other faiths " by the fact that
in it everything is related to the redemption accomplished by Jesus of Nazareth." [1]   Christian faith, then,
is a feeling of absolute dependence in relation to this
redemption ; but if that is so, it seems impossible at
first sight to find any room whatsoever for a systematic
study such as theology.   At this point, it looks as if,
having severed the connection of theology with the
general investigation into " the nature and substance of
things ", Schleiermacher had cut it off from every possible subject-matter.   But of course Schleiermacher tried
to extract himself from this difficulty by a bold expedient,
namely, by affirming that " Christian doctrines are
accounts of the Christian religious affections set forth
in speech." [2]   " The doctrines in all their forms have
their ultimate ground so exclusively in the emotions of
the religious self-consciousness, that where these do not
exist the doctrines cannot arise." [3]   Even where the
" purely scientific activity " gives rise to " propositions
of speculative import about the Supreme Being which
. . . are . . . difficult to distinguish from the corresponding propositions which arose purely out of reflection upon the religious emotions," a distinction must
none the less be drawn, for " dogmatic propositions
never make their original appearance except in trains
of thought which have received their impulse from

---

[1] Schleiermacher, *The Christian Faith*, p. 52.
[2] *Ibid.*, p. 76.   [3] *Ibid.*, p. 78.

religious moods of mind." [1]   Thus in theology Schleiermacher is not directly concerned with revelation but
with faith, piety, the feeling of absolute dependence,
and with its modifications ; and if we wonder how
from such a starting-point and subject-matter Schleiermacher is able to evolve the traditional doctrines of the
Christian faith, the answer is that he cannot do so
without reference to the beliefs actually received within
the Christian community.   These are held to be transcripts or reports of communal piety, but in the last
resort this can only be regarded as a sheer assumption.
If the assumption is granted, the task of dogmatics may
then " be defined as that of giving an orderly and
articulate view of the doctrines received in a specific
Church at a specific time." [2]   But, as H. R. Mackintosh
says,[3] this will not stand examination.   Dogmatics

is supremely interested not in what has been believed, or even
in what is believed now, but in what ought to be believed by
those to whom God has spoken in Revelation.   As a norma-
tive discipline, it brings a certain standard of truth to bear
upon the preaching or the confessions of the Church, and,
in the light of this standard—the Word of God—it puts past
and present alike on trial.

It is clear that in his emphasis upon piety or feeling
Schleiermacher is forcing the doctrines of the Christian
faith into an alien mould ; but this error cannot be
allowed to obscure the fundamental contribution of a
great theologian.   Theology, he has taught us, is not
the science of God.   It is concerned with religion, and
is indeed religion reflecting upon itself and seeking to
understand itself.   When faith is identified with feeling
this concept of theology implies, or is made to imply
in the hands of Schleiermacher, that the theological task
is to present systematically the beliefs upheld in a given
Christian community, to show how they arise from its

[1] *Ibid.*, p. 82.   [2] H. R. Mackintosh, *Types of Modern Theology*, p. 62.
[3] *Ibid.*, p. 62.

communal piety and to display their connection, one
with another.   If, however, this specific idea of the task
of theology proves itself untenable, it remains to be seen
whether the general concept of theology which it articu-
lates cannot be worked out more defensibly in some
other way.   And this in fact is what the main movement
of Christian theology has been doing ever since.

Thus for Ritschl, too, theology arises in and only in
the community of faith ; but faith is no longer regarded
as mere feeling, even as the feeling of absolute dependence.   Agreeing with Schleiermacher in his general
approach to the matter Ritschl, none the less decisively,
set aside the other's specific and peculiar articulation of
the theme.

> Authentic and complete knowledge of Jesus' religious sig-
> nificance—His significance, that is, as a Founder of religion
> —depends, then, on one's reckoning oneself part of the
> community which He founded, and this precisely in so far
> as it believes itself to have received the forgiveness of sins as
> His peculiar gift ; [1]

and in adopting this particular standpoint Ritschl is
reaffirming the typical modern approach to the subject.
" We are able," he says,[2] " to know and understand
God, sin, conversion, eternal life, in the Christian sense,
only so far as we consciously and intentionally reckon
ourselves members of the community which Christ has
founded."

> System proper must all the more certainly be conditioned
> by the fact that every part of theological knowledge is con-
> strued from the standpoint of the Christian community, since
> only so can the worth of Christ as Revealer be employed
> throughout, as the basis of knowledge in solving all the
> problems of theology.[3]

But, in spite of this large and fundamental agreement,
Ritschl could not accept the central and ultimate place

---

[1] A. Ritschl, *Justification and Reconciliation* (T. & T. Clark, 1900), p. 2.
[2] *Ibid.*, p. 4.   [3] *Ibid.*, p. 6.

accorded by Schleiermacher to feeling, and to feeling more than anything else.[1] In its stead, he put the consciousness of value as a concept more adequate to the reality of faith ; and in doing so he was not simply substituting one possible factor for another, he was turning his back decisively upon what the other involved. For to put all the emphasis upon feeling, as Schleiermacher did, is to open the door wide to subjectivism ; it is to necessitate some such description of Christian doctrines as Schleiermacher was compelled to give when he described them as transcripts of religious affections ; and it is to shut one's eyes to the reality of God as He has revealed Himself in Jesus Christ. Ritschl was entirely at one with Schleiermacher in " claiming that religion has an independence of its own, and that it is to the religious man himself we must go, not to the philosopher weaving theories about him, if his believing life is to be understood ".[2] But, if this is so, Ritschl also insists, and no less vigorously, that religious faith is not just a feature of man's life which begins and ends in man but a relationship to, an awareness of, God ; it is not to be equated to blind feeling, but throws in its lot with our open consciousness of something outside and beyond.

This, it must be admitted, is a much more adequate articulation of the characteristic general approach of modern theology, but the question remains whether it is completely adequate. And the answer to this question reveals a curious contrast between Schleiermacher and Ritschl. There is no doubt that in some sense the former's achievement greatly exceeded his promise and prospect, for, unhopeful as his start might be in respect of his concentration upon feeling, he did contrive to introduce into his system what were, by and large, the traditional doctrines of the Christian faith, and he did so by attending to the beliefs actually received in a given Christian community, and by relating them,

[1] Cf. ibid., p. 587.　　[2] Mackintosh, Types of Modern Theology, p. 149.

perhaps forcibly, to the pure feeling out of which they were supposed to arise. Ritschl, on the other hand, was able to start with a more adequate promise and prospect, with more adequate and promising presuppositions, in particular with a more adequate identification of faith ; for, whatever else it might be, it was for Ritschl a conscious relationship to " Christ as Revealer." This consciousness Ritschl further described as a consciousness of value, and so the basis of theological knowledge became " the *worth* of Christ as Revealer." But, if Schleiermacher's achievement exceeded his promise, Ritschl's achievement, in elaborating this fundamental theme, fell considerably short of his promise, for there is no doubt that in his hands " the demands, the outlook, the standards or prepossessions of the moral man are allowed to lay down the law to the believing mind, and to forbid it to grasp in their fulness the transcendent new truths and gifts that God is offering in Christ." [1]   It is pre-eminently in this respect that the Ritschlian theology falls short, for in it the revelation of God in Christ is unwittingly watered down and brought within the compass of our ordinary unredeemed consciousness of value.

The question now arises how the most recent developments in theology, and, in particular, how the movement of Barthianism, may be understood in relation to this development which we have traced within the characteristically modern approach to theology. Perhaps no better starting-point for such an inquiry could be found than a summary provided by the late Professor H. R. Mackintosh. Speaking and writing in the decade which eventually saw the outbreak of the second World War, Mackintosh expressed the matter thus:

> It is now some years [he said][2] since Ritschl's great successor, Karl Barth, stepped into the arena ; and that Barth is definitely a more Christian thinker than Ritschl no one, I

---

[1] Mackintosh, *Types of Modern Theology*, p. 173.   [2] *Ibid.*, p. 173.

should suppose, can doubt who takes revelation seriously. But in declared intention and programme the two theologians are much nearer to each other than has often been supposed. The difference may, perhaps, be shortly put thus : that Ritschl undertakes to furnish a theology inspired throughout by Scripture, but too often fails to keep his promise, whereas Barth is set upon thinking out something that will deserve to be called a " Theology of the Word of God ", and has so far proceeded with a consistency and power which is engaging the attention of the whole Christian Church. It is in performance, not in chosen aim, that the two men stand so far apart.

In this verdict, it must be allowed, there is important truth. For one thing, the Barthian theology is not hesitant in accepting the view that theology can take place only within the area or community of faith, and in that respect Dr. Barth stands firmly in the principal line of development which is characteristic of modern theology. At the outset of his *Church Dogmatics* he affirms clearly and succinctly that " theology is a function of the Church." [1] Dogmatics is certainly a work of human knowledge demanding the intellectual and mental qualities which all such work demands, but above all " it presupposes Christian faith, which even in the deepest and purest surrender to this task in itself does not by any means just happen. In fact dogmatics is a function of the Christian Church." [2] In the second place, Dr. Barth is in complete agreement with Ritschl, as against Schleiermacher, that faith is not a matter of feeling or of any of the modes of feeling, whether it be a feeling of absolute dependence or any other. In fact subjectivism here is quite out of the question. In faith we are concerned not with ourselves but with God, with His revelation of Himself in Jesus Christ His Son. " Dogmatics is a function of the Christian Church " and " to the Church is given the promise of the criterion for Christian faith, namely, the revelation of God." [3]

[1] *The Doctrine of the Word of God*, p. 1.
[2] *Ibid.*, p. 18.   [3] *Ibid.*, p. 18.

Indeed, " the essence of the Church is Jesus Christ," [1] and

> thus we assert that dogmatics presupposes faith, presupposes the determination of human action through listening, and as obedience to the essence of the Church ; whence we assert that at every step and proposition it presupposes the free grace of God, which may from time to time be given or else refused, as the object and meaning of this human action.[2]

No-one could lay greater stress upon revelation than Dr. Barth has done, and so far it is true to say that with regard to their intentions he and Ritschl stand very close to each other. Theology falls within the area of faith, and faith is in some sense an openness to the revelation of God.

But, given such extensive and significant agreement, divergences no less significant may even yet appear, and that so far as intention, and not just achievement, is concerned. Faith is an openness to the revelation of God. In faith man is related to the revelation of God, to Jesus Christ as the way, the truth and the life, as Lord and Saviour. Theology can only occur in relation to this relation—at least theology as it is understood for the most part by the modern mind. But the question arises whether theology takes its stand on the human side of the relationship, or on the divine. To that question, as it happens, Ritschl has a very definite reply which he gives in an important passage.

> Dogmatics [he says][3] comprehends all religious processes in man under the category of Divine grace, that is, it looks at them from the standpoint of God. But it is, of course, impossible so thoroughly to maintain this standpoint in our experience, as thereby to obtain complete knowledge of the operations of grace. For the standpoint of our knowledge lies in formal opposition to God. Only for an instant can we transfer ourselves to the Divine standpoint. A theology, therefore, which consisted of nothing but propositions of this

---

[1] *The Doctrine of the Word of God*, p. 16.   [2] *Ibid.*, p. 19.
[3] *Justification and Reconciliation*, pp. 34f.

stamp could never be understood, and would be composed of words which really did not express knowledge on our part. If what is wanted is to write theology on the plan not merely of a narrative of the great deeds done by God, but of a system representing the salvation He has wrought out, then we must exhibit the operations of God—justification, regeneration, the communication of the Holy Spirit, the bestowal of blessedness in the *summum bonum*—in such a way as shall involve an analysis of the corresponding voluntary activities in which man appropriates the operations of God. This method has been already adopted by Schleiermacher. Now those who are strangers to the work of theology urge against this method, that what they are concerned about is the objective bearing of theological doctrines and not the interpretation of them as reflected in the subject, and that this method renders the whole matter uncertain. Such a view is at variance with the right theory of knowledge ; for in knowledge we observe and explain even the objects of sense-perception, not as they are in themselves, but as we perceive them. If what is intended in Dogmatics is merely to describe objectively Divine operations, that means the abandonment of the attempt to understand their practical bearing. For apart from voluntary activity, through which we receive and utilise for our own blessedness the operations of God, we have no means of understanding objective dogmas as religious truths. Objective knowledge in this region is disinterested knowledge. Such knowledge, it is true, is quite in place in natural science ; but in theology, however coolly we may sketch out its formal relations, we have to do with spiritual processes of such a kind that our salvation depends on them.

By this Ritschl means, amongst other things, that while in theology we are concerned throughout with God's grace, it is we who are concerned, and who are concerned not as givers of grace but as its recipients, as those who are apprehended and not as He who apprehends. In theology we are in *formal* opposition to God, for in faith we are, not against God—on the contrary, we are for Him who is so finally for us—but we are over against Him ; we are not God. In faith we do not look over God's shoulders, we look up all the time to His outstretched arms, outstretched in mercy towards us ; and in theology we cannot reverse the standpoint of faith.   How right Ritschl is in this passage !

Yet Dr. Barth could not accept it as it stands, especially the statement that theology must involve " an analysis of the corresponding voluntary activities in which man appropriates the operations of God."   Does it, then, follow that, in spite of the obvious objections, Barthianism takes its stand on the *divine* side of the relationship between man and God, not on the human side like Ritschl ?   Although some slender justification for such an opinion might be found, not in any precise statement made by Dr. Barth, but in the general impression that his theology sometimes leaves of intransigence and dogmatism, especially in his frequent assumption that any departure from his own position is a betrayal of evangelical truth, this verdict cannot be long sustained.   If it were true, it would mean that theology would be by the very nature of the case infallible, and this, Dr. Barth believes, is true of no theology, and certainly not of his own.

> Dogmatics [he tells us][1] . . . must be an inquiry.   It knows the light that is perfect in itself, that discovers all in a flash.   But it knows it only in the prism of this act, which, however radically or existentially it may be regarded, is a human act, offering in itself no sort of surety for the correctness of the appropriation in question, being rather fallible and therefore itself in need of criticism and revision, of repeated and ever closer re-testing.

" The givenness of the special and decisive conditions of dogmatics, the decision from time to time of what is or is not the truth in dogmatics, are matters of divine predestination."[2]   " Without exception the act of faith (*i.e.* its basis in divine predestination, the free act of God on man and his work) is the condition which renders dogmatic work possible, by which also it is called in question in deadly earnest." [3]   So far further, then, Dr. Barth

---

[1] *The Doctrine of the Word of God*, p. 14.
[2] *Ibid.*, pp. 22f.   [3] *Ibid.*, p. 23.

and Ritschl are at one, since for both theology takes its stand, and must take its stand, on the human side of the relationship of faith.

Once that has been said, however, an important difference must immediately be noted. For Ritschl activity is present and in evidence on the human side as well as on the divine, but for Barthianism that is not plainly so. Indeed Dr. Barth declares [1] that " faith is the determination of human action by the essence of the Church, that is by Jesus Christ, by the gracious approach of God to man," and it is clear that he means the complete determination of human action. " Truth of revelation is the freely acting God, Himself and quite alone." [2] It is true that even here Dr. Barth speaks of human *action*, and by this action he seems to mean mere listening, a sheer openness, a complete receptivity ; and although he finds the cause of human insecurity and fallibility in this matter in what he calls " the intractability of faith and its object ",[3] he affirms a little later that " dogmatics receives the measure with which it measures in an act of human appropriation." [4] It would be idle to deny that at this point Dr. Barth's thought is not easy, that if it is not confused it is at any rate complicated ; and yet nothing, or almost nothing, could be more important for the understanding of his whole theology than the understanding of it at this very place. It is here that there arises that curious combination of intransigence and fallibility, of apparent infallibility, in other words, with a really admitted possibility of error, of arrogance, one might say, with a deep humility, which is on the formal side the hallmark of the whole system. It is clearly and characteristically Dr. Barth who is speaking when it is said of dogmatics that

in human uncertainty, like any other science, it establishes the most certain truth which long ago came to light. As a

---

[1] *Ibid.*, p. 18.   [2] *Ibid.*, p. 16.   [3] *Ibid.*, p. 12.   [4] *Ibid.*, p. 14.

statement of faith every statement in dogmatics, in view of its peculiar object, must be ventured upon in the certainty that it expresses not human but divine truth ; it must not avoid by a hair's breadth the rigour of the " dogmatic " (as distinguished from the academic reserve of a philosophical proposition). . . . The intractability of faith and its object should and will see to it that divine certainty cannot become human security.[1]

What is the explanation ? It is that for Dr. Barth human reason in faith is completely determined by divine grace, the truth of faith is " given ", and when error occurs in dogmatics it can only be because the truth was not given and human reason of itself has offered human error for divine truth. These indeed, on this view, are the only possibilities in dogmatics, divine truth or human error. There is no such thing here as human truth—if Dr. Barth is right. But can it seriously be maintained that there is no difference in respect of human truth between one dogmatic system and another ? May not two men who are altogether one in faith none the less give different accounts, the one more adequate, the other less adequate, of this relationship of faith in which they both stand ? And, if they endeavour to give systematic expression to this faith which they have in common, may they not differ, in greater or less degree, in the order in which they present the various dogmatic topics, and may not one order be more adequate than another ? And, if the answer to these two questions is in the affirmative, as it seems bound to be, must we not say that in dogmatic theology there may be an element of human truth as well as human error, that besides false opinion human reason may also deliver judgments which are true, while working of course within the area of grace and faith ?

[1] *The Doctrine of the Word of God*, p. 12. Is this statement itself which professes to be true divinely certain ? Is it also simply and completely given ? This question which arises for Barthianism corresponds to the question whether the radical empiricist's principle of empirical verifiability is itself empirically verifiable.

The truth is that Dr. Barth has his own peculiar
concept of faith, and that out of it there arises his own
peculiar idea of dogmatic theology. If in faith, as he
maintains, we are not only confronted by God in Christ,
but are completely determined by His grace on every
side of our being, including our reason, then it follows
that, although it is a Person, rather than propositions,
that is revealed, propositions are nevertheless *also* revealed, and are an essential part of the revelation, so
that " divine certain knowledge " is " given." And,
further, it follows that when the man of faith undertakes the work of dogmatic theology, there is only one
course open to him, or rather there are two, for he may
choose to speculate blindly about this hard impenetrable
fact, this complete determination of his being from without—a course which Dr. Barth firmly and properly
eschews—or else he may content himself with reporting
(in some systematic order which presumably is not given)
the " divine certain knowledge " which is given to faith,
the contents, in other words, of this complete determination.   Indeed, it is far from clear whether on Dr. Barth's
view dogmatics is the human report of this divine knowledge or this divine knowledge itself. Thus he can
make two statements about dogmatics which do not go
well together, for he can say that dogmatics " presupposes Christian faith " and that " dogmatics is only
possible as an act of faith, in the determination of human
action by listening, and as obedience towards Jesus
Christ." [1] That the individual dogmatician should
follow such a calling may well be an act of faith and
of obedience towards Jesus Christ, but what Dr. Barth
would have us believe is that dogmatics, and not just
dogmatising, is an act of faith ; whereas, in truth,
dogmatising, besides being an act of faith and obedience,
is an act of reflection upon faith, and *dogmatics* is the
result of such an action.   How else is it that naturally
and inherently and not just by an artificial convention

[1] *Ibid.*, p. 18.

dogmatics refers to God in the third person and not the second ?

Moreover, it is because of his theory of the complete determination of reason in faith and the peculiar idea of dogmatic theology which it yields that Dr. Barth can regard dogmatics as the test of proclamation and preaching, as its criticism and revision.   Church proclamation has a real responsibility, and " its real responsibility arises out of its intention to be proclamation of the Word of God " ; [1] but, that being so, there is always a question whether and how far that intention is fulfilled. Christian preaching, professing to be proclamation of the Word of God, is under attack from the living Word of God Himself.   But, says Dr. Barth, " the attack on her, *i.e.* the Church, from God's side demands something to correspond on man's side, *i.e.* human conscientiousness and investigation," [2] and that is provided by dogmatics.   " The possibility of putting the dogmatic question, the possibility of dogmatic criticism and revision, arises out of the claim with which language about God comes forward in the Church, and out of the atmosphere of expectation with which it is there surrounded." [3]   " Dogmatics is the servant of preaching, because it raises this question.   It tests the ' orthodoxy' of contemporary kerygma." [4]   " In being an exposition, it is also an investigation and a polemic, a criticism and a revision." [5]   " Proclamation must exist as the execution of the divine behest to the Church. Dogmatics must exist, because proclamation is fallible human work." [6]   " The datum from which dogmatics starts is neither God, nor revelation, nor faith.   This is the datum from which proclamation starts. . . ." [7] The datum from which dogmatics starts is " a different one, namely the debatable fact that in proclamation by

---

[1] *The Doctrine of the Word of God*, p. 80.   [2] *Ibid.*, p. 83.
[3] *Ibid.*, p. 86.   [4] *Ibid.*, p. 92.   [5] *Ibid.*, p. 92.
[6] *Ibid.*, p. 91.   [7] *Ibid.*, p. 91.

men there is human language about God, revelation, faith. . . ." [1]

Two possible misunderstandings, however, must be avoided. For one thing, it is not to be supposed that dogmatics ever reaches a state of finality. Each new day must raise for itself the dogmatic question. Secondly, and even more important, Dr. Barth makes it quite plain that " as compared with Church proclamation dogmatics cannot have access to a higher, better source of knowledge." [2] It knows of no norm which is not already accessible to faith, and Dr. Barth explicitly rejects the attempt to make the word of Apostles and Prophets into such an external yardstick. Once again there is presented the curious but characteristic combination of fallibility and infallibility, a combination which we have already found perplexing. For what kind of test can it be which offers no yardstick, no norm of its own to apply to that which is tested ? If it were Dr. Barth's opinion that dogmatics had exclusive access to a standard by which proclamation might be tested his position would be untenable but intelligible, but there seems no justification for speaking so firmly of a test, in the absence of such a standard. On the other hand, it quickly appears that, just as the norm or test has disappeared, so also has the proclamation which is to be tested, for dogmatics, we are told, does not concern itself directly with the preaching of yesterday but with *its* dogmatics which did, and that, presumably, with an earlier dogmatics, and so on, until proclamation as that which is to be tested is lost in an indefinite regress. Indeed, except by a fiction, it was never there.

What then has led Dr. Barth to this simplified conception of dogmatics as the test of Christian preaching ? It is, once again, his view of faith as a *complete determination* of our being by the revelation of God, and the implication that in faith and in dogmatics there are only two possibilities, divine truth and human error. In this

---

[1] *Ibid.*, p. 92.   [2] *Ibid.*, p. 93.

connection there is a significant passage in which Dr.
Barth quotes the verdict of Paul Althaus that

> theology means the completion of the act of faith in the
> sphere of thought.   Faith ought to overcome the world.
> Theology is the wrestling to overcome the world of spirits
> and of thoughts.   Theologians thereby achieve reflection
> . . . as a service to the whole community, and therefore, so
> to speak, as a service in representative thinking.

Having made this quotation, Dr. Barth goes on to add
his own comment in the form of a question, " In spite
of and in face of this detailed definition, would it not
be ascribing too much to theology, to make a thing
which is promised only to faith as such (which in that
case may also be the faith of a ' layman ') the goal of
its ' wrestling ' ? " [1]   Dr. Barth could hardly have come
nearer to admitting that, on his account of revelation,
what is given to faith is neither propositions by themselves, nor a Person by Himself, but propositions and
Person together.

While it is true, then, as H. R. Mackintosh suggested,
that, starting with similar intentions, Ritschl and Dr.
Barth differ greatly in their achievements, since the
former failed and the latter has largely succeeded in
providing an evangelical theology, one in which the
revelation of God is the governing factor, there is a
great deal more to be said than that.   Like Schleiermacher and Ritschl, Dr. Barth has taken up his theological standpoint within the area of faith, within the
relationship of man to God created by the revelation in
Jesus Christ.   Like Schleiermacher and Ritschl, also,
in spite of stray impressions which he may leave to the
contrary, Dr. Barth's standpoint is on the human side
of that relationship.   Where else indeed could it be ?
Moreover, like Ritschl, he regards faith, not as blind
feeling, but as an openness to revelation.   On the other
hand, where Ritschl in effect tended to regard our
human consciousness of value, not just as a guiding

[1] *The Doctrine of the Word of God*, p. 93.

interpretative principle in understanding what is revealed, but as a regulative and governing principle
instead, Dr. Barth rejects or tries to reject both regulative
and interpretative principles altogether and so to portray
faith as a sheer openness to revelation. Where Ritschl
allowed an interpretative principle to become a regulative one, Dr. Barth in ruling out the regulative principle
rejected it also as an interpretative one and came to
regard faith as a pure receptivity, a sheer openness to
revelation, involving reason, but reason completely
determined by the Word of God, reason not as a
power, capacity or activity, but as a passivity, a mere
location, a blank page upon which marks might be
made.

Even if this odd conception of faith could be maintained it can fairly be argued that Dr. Barth ought to
have distinguished more clearly between faith and theology. " Lord, I believe ; help thou mine unbelief "
—that is the voice of faith, not theology. " I believe
in God . . ."—that is the beginning of a theology which
presupposes faith. In faith we are addressed by God
and we speak to Him in return ; in theology there is
language about God, revelation and faith, just as there
is such language, on Dr. Barth's own admission, in proclamation. There is a clear distinction here which
ought to be made, for quite manifestly the object of our
faith is God, God as He revealed Himself to us in Jesus
Christ His Son, and not credal statements or dogmatic
systems—these may change but God is the same yesterday, today and for ever. There is a plain distinction
here which ought to be made ; but it ought to be made
simply and solely for the sake of clear thinking and
certainly not for the division and departmentalisation of
personal life. There is a plain distinction also between
moral experience and ethical theory, but the distinction
does not alter the fact that in pursuing ethical theory
the moralist may at the same time be doing his duty.
In exactly the same way the theologian in his theological

work may be acting in faith and obedience to Jesus
Christ ; but that fact should not obscure the other fact
that at the same time, as a theologian doing his theological work, he is thinking and speaking systematically
about God, revelation and faith.   Dr. Barth has drawn
a curiously rigid distinction between proclamation and
dogmatics, a distinction which he is able to maintain
only by a fiction, and he has obscured what seems to
be a very plain distinction between faith and dogmatics,
between faith and theology.   Even if faith is to be
regarded as a sheer openness to revelation, a pure
receptivity, that distinction is still valid, and dogmatic
theology would then appear, not as thinking or reflection
about God, revelation and faith, but as a bare human
report of the divinely certain knowledge implanted in
the mind of man by the revelation of God in the complete
determination by the one of the other.

The conception of faith, however, as a sheer openness
to revelation, as pure receptivity, cannot be maintained.
There are indeed two aspects of the matter which require
serious criticism, namely, the hidden logic by which
Dr. Barth arrives at the conception and the conception
itself.   Thus, so far as the hidden logic of Barthianism
is concerned, we have already found reason to suppose
that this whole theology is governed throughout by a
preconception in which God is posited as *fundamentally*
Creator and man is portrayed as *mere* creature.   In
harmony with this idea grace is conceived as a complete
determining of man's being by God, as a creating out
of nothing ; while revelation, in turn, is regarded as
sheerly and completely given to man along with its
appropriate response in faith, and consequently it has
to be considered not as revelation in a Person only but
as revelation in a Person along with propositions.   This,
however, is not a true account of our human situation,
and it is certainly not the Biblical account.   The God
of the Bible is not predominantly Creator but is equally
Ruler, Governor, King, and Father ; while its men are

not *mere* creatures but human beings who were created for a purpose. Thus in his reaction from Ritschl, Dr. Barth has not succeeded in rejecting all regulative and interpretative principles ; he has his own principle of interpretation, not an ethical one like Ritschl's, but a metaphysical one—a principle of interpretation, moreover, which can find no adequate support either in reason or in revelation.

In the second place, the conception of faith to which this hidden logic leads is also questionable. If revelation and the response of faith are completely given and sheerly created by grace, then all that the word " faith " can connote on the human side is a bare openness to revelation, an empty space, a blank page, a pure receptivity. But to treat faith in this way is not to raise it above the level of our ordinary rational and moral activities, it is rather to reduce it below the threshold of personal and spiritual life, below the level of sense-experience, in which, as Kant pointed out, understanding as well as sensibility is already at work. To treat faith thus, as a bare openness to something sheerly given, is to rule out at once that element of personal spontaneity without which conviction, trust, loyalty, obedience and love would not be what they are. In his endeavour to exalt revelation Dr. Barth has overleaped himself and taken away the means whereby in human life, in human faith, the revelation can be exalted. In his anxiety to deprive me of any misplaced credit for the fact that I believe in Christ he has theologically destroyed the fact that none the less it is I who believe in Christ who first of all believed in me. The truth is that faith as conviction, as trust, as loyalty, as obedience, as love, cannot be completely determined ; there is an ineradicable element of personal spontaneity, without which the conviction, loyalty and love would not be mine—or anyone's—and would not therefore be conviction, loyalty and love.

Moreover, to point to another side of the same fact,

we cannot have conviction in respect of something
sheerly given to us ; we cannot have trust, loyalty,
obedience and love towards it. A yellow patch which
is sheerly given to the senses arouses no conviction whatsoever. In order that there shall be conviction, loyalty
and love, what is given to me must strike home, must
arouse understanding, must evoke appreciation. It
must make contact positively and negatively with the
man I am, with my hopes and fears, my illusions and
beliefs, my virtues and my sins. And if what is given
is the revelation of God in Christ and if the result in
me is faith in Christ there is something of me in that
faith, it is *my* faith, it is coloured by my mind and by
the mind of the age in which I live ; but it is at the
same time faith *in Christ* and it is the gift of God's grace.
Thus there is already thought and understanding in
faith ; and, although the distinction between theology
and faith is still valid, it is again clear that this distinction does not divide and departmentalise the personal
life. For, as we have already seen, not only may the
dogmatising of the theologian be an act of faith and
obedience towards Jesus Christ, but also as thinking and
reflection it is continuous with faith which already involves thought. In theology faith seeks to understand
itself, to exhibit its inner logic, which is not, however, a
humanly self-contained logic but a movement of man's
mind and spirit in response to the revelation of God
in Christ. There is even a dialectic connected with
this logic, though it is not a logical dialectic between
objective statements of faith but a living dialectic between
subject and Subject, between the truth as it is in Christ
and our inadequate, fallible conceptions of it.

Here the argument has passed from criticism to construction, to the indication of an alternative to Barthianism within the strictly evangelical field, an alternative
which by contrast is thoroughly ethical in its intention.
Such an alternative is born in the admission that in
faith we understand, we see through a glass darkly ;

we also do more than see, but we do see and understand, not along the lines of an understanding which
might be open to us apart from revelation and grace—
quite definitely not that—but along the lines of an
understanding to which we have been quickened by
God's confronting us in grace in the Person of Jesus
Christ His Son.   No doubt Dr. Barth, too, can speak
of natural reason as quickened and enlightened, but he
uses these terms in so radical a sense that they come to
refer to nothing short of a complete determination from
without.   Even Dr. Brunner's rigid dichotomy of form
and content is inadequate to describe the ethical evangelical relationship of faith, for there is no reason to suppose
that every natural judgment is condemned by revelation
as either false or irrelevant.   What is true is that all
such judgments are given a new context, the context of
God's sovereign grace, in which doubtless they are transformed.   In faith we understand and, let it be admitted,
in faith we also misunderstand.   In faith there is human
truth and human error ; but in faith both the truth and
the error are seeking to comprehend the truth of God,
as it is in Christ.

It follows also that theology itself appears in a somewhat different light and bears a rather different slant.
It is still possible, and indeed necessary, to maintain the
valuable negative side of Dr. Barth's position, that
theology does not just presuppose the Church and faith
but relates itself to the day-to-day life and existence of
the Church and does not aim at " an independent theory,
gnosis, or speculation, remote from her action." [1]   On
the positive side, however, two things must be said.   It
must be affirmed that what theology achieves has in
some way an existence independent of the act by which
it is achieved, and as such it may, by God's grace,
become the vehicle of divine truth.   Secondly, it is no
longer possible to think of theology as something sheerly
given to—or withheld from—the Church as the rigid

[1] *The Doctrine of the Word of God*, p. 94.

test of her preaching. It is rather the critical self-understanding of faith, *where faith is clearly and unambiguously the response in man to the revelation of God in Christ,* and as such it is a contribution, from the sphere of thought within the Church, towards the clarification of her message and her mission. It is itself proclamation, self-critical and systematic proclamation, of the truth as it is in Christ, so far as it has been given to faith to apprehend it.

CHAPTER VIII

THE BIBLICAL SITUATION

THE Bible is in some sense the Word of God. We do not attempt to prove this. There is no need even if it were possible. It proves itself, for the Bible authenticates itself to heart and conscience as the Word of God. But, when we reflect upon this, we are compelled for the sake of clarity to distinguish two senses in which the Bible is the Word of God. It is the record of, and witness to, God's Word spoken to men and women of other times and it is also the vehicle of God's Word spoken to us in our time. Reflection compels us in the interests of clarity to draw this distinction, and the Bible itself illustrates it. Perhaps it does so nowhere more clearly than in the account it gives of a controversy between David the king and Nathan the prophet. It happened that when David was king he fell in love with Bathsheba, the wife of Uriah, one of the king's soldiers ; and David arranged that in the heat of battle, at the most dangerous part of the line, Uriah would be killed. Then, with Uriah out of the way, David took Bathsheba as his wife. But, we are told, the thing that David had done displeased the Lord, and Nathan the prophet was sent to him with a message, with a parable, a word from the Lord. There were two men, said Nathan, in one city, the one rich and the other poor. As the king listened attentively, the prophet went on. The rich man had exceeding many flocks and herds, but the poor man had nothing save one little ewe lamb which he had bought and nourished. And it grew up together with him and with his children ; it did eat of his own morsel, and drank of his own cup, and lay in his bosom, and was unto him as a daughter. Now there came a traveller to the rich man, but he, as

rich men sometimes do, hesitated to take of his own
flock and his own herd to prepare for the wayfarer. Instead, he took the poor man's lamb and dressed it for
the man that was come to him.

Such was Nathan's message, his word from the Lord
to David, spoken in the form of a narrative like the
Bible as a whole ; and the reader can scarcely miss its
point. Behind the figures of those two men who dwelt
in one city, the one rich and the other poor, he can
plainly discern the shadows of two other people, one a
king and the other a soldier in the king's army. And
behind the figure of the single ewe lamb in the parable
he can detect the shadow of the soldier's wife, Bathsheba. But the important question concerns the understanding and reaction of David. How did he take it ?
Was he filled with shame ? Was he stricken by conscience, and by a higher voice than conscience, the
remonstrance of Almighty God ? On the contrary,
David was angry. His anger was kindled greatly, we
are told, against the rich man ; and the king said to
Nathan, As the Lord liveth, the man that hath done this
is worthy to die, and he shall restore the lamb fourfold,
because he did this thing and because he had no pity.
David was filled and overflowing with indignation against
the man. But, said Nathan, *thou* art the man. Thus
saith the Lord, the God of Israel, I anointed thee king
over Israel, and I delivered thee out of the hand of Saul,
and I gave thee thy master's house and thy master's
wives and the house of Israel and of Judah ; and if that
had been too little I would have added unto thee such
and such things. Wherefore, then, hast thou despised
the word of the Lord to do that which is evil in His
sight ?

Now this incident clearly necessitates a distinction
between two different understandings of Nathan's parable, for, manifestly, David did understand from the
beginning what was said to him, and yet it is also true
that, hearing, he heard but did not at first understand.

What is involved in this fact is a distinction between what we shall call a merely narrative understanding of the parable and an understanding of it which can be described as addressive, clamant, literally urgent. The distinction is in some ways similar to, but not identical with, that between indicative and imperative moods. The latter is a distinction between two linguistic forms which are mutually exclusive, in the sense that a sentence which is in the indicative mood is by that very fact not in the imperative mood and *vice versa*, whereas the former distinction is one between two uses and understandings of language, which are not so clearly exclusive of each other. Of course the distinction between language and its understanding must not be pressed too far, for apart from some understanding language is simply a noise or a succession of noises, which would not permit even of the differentiation of verbal moods. On the one hand, there is a formal or abstract understanding of language which takes no account of the particular situation of utterance, which is concerned only with the actual fact of utterance claiming attention. On the other hand, there is a material understanding which does relate it to the particular situation in question. It is within this latter understanding that the distinction arises between a merely narrative and a clamant understanding of language. In other words, we are concerned here with a distinction, not within language merely as an instrument of communication, but within the use of this instrument. The inherent function of all language is to communicate, to convey information, although it cannot be assumed that its original function was that only ; and even if a piece of language were to consist as nearly as possible of a bare imperative it would still convey information, for example, about the wishes of the person using it, for unless it did so it could not fulfil any other purpose. If this is true, all language is narrative, in our sense of the word, although it may not all make use of a non-imperative mood. But if all

language is narrative it is certainly not all merely narrative ; some language is clamant, it is, as we have said,
literally urgent ; it is used to lay a claim upon the person
to whom it is addressed, although, as we have seen, in
doing that it does not forsake its inherent function of
being narrative and informative, and it may even proceed
by means of the indicative mood.

There is, then, a distinction between a narrative and
a clamant understanding of language ; and this distinction enables us to understand David's encounter
with Nathan. David's initial mistake was not simply
that he misunderstood the parable. He understood it
well enough as narrative, it conveyed a message to his
conscience, and, indeed, unless it had done so he could
not even have misunderstood it. But he did misunderstand it as merely narrative ; he failed to see that he
himself was being confronted, addressed, rebuked and
claimed by God. That was the very essence of his
error, and it was that which distinguished his first understanding of the situation from his last. It was certainly
not true that one understanding was a total misunderstanding in comparison with the other ; nor was it true
that the earlier understanding was spectatorial and dispassionate, for it is clear that it was not so. The difference lay in David's awareness (or lack of it) that a claim
was being made upon him and made upon him by a
higher Power than man's. The difference, in other
words, was exactly that between a merely narrative and
a clamant understanding of the message ; and to find it
elsewhere is to mistake incidentals for essentials.

A similar treatment may be extended to the parables
of Jesus, and He Himself seems to invite and suggest it
when He warns that those who hear them may indeed
hear, but not understand. There are two quite different
but not unrelated ways in which these parables may be
understood. We may hear in them Jesus talking about
God, or God in Christ talking to us—our understanding
of them may be merely narrative or clamant and literally

urgent. " A certain man had two sons ; and the younger of them said to his father, Father, give me the portion of goods that falleth to me . . . and the younger son . . . took his journey into a far country." What do we make of that ? Who is this younger son ? Is he just a hypothetical figure, a purely imaginary person-ality introduced to offset the character of God ? Or is he rather a real person, much nearer home to ourselves ? May it be indeed that I am the man ? " And when he came to himself he said . . . I will arise and go to my Father, and will say unto him, Father, I have sinned against heaven and before thee, and am no more worthy to be called thy son. . . ." Once again, is it a hypo-thetical character who speaks or someone real ? " But when he was yet a great way off, his father saw him, and had compassion, and ran, and fell on his neck, and kissed him . . . and . . . said . . . This my son was dead, and is alive again ; he was lost and is found. . . ." What do we make of it now ? Is this a wholly imaginary situation and an entirely fictitious son, devised by the mind of Christ to display the character of God ? Or is it something more, is it actually our situation, is God Himself speaking to us ?

Plainly, there are two understandings of Christ's parables, and the difference between them is the one we have already acknowledged between a merely narra-tive understanding and one that is clamant, addressive, literally urgent. Indeed, this distinction applies to the Bible in its entirety. In one sense it is merely narrative, it tells us about God, about His Word spoken to men and women of other times, and about those to whom it was spoken. In this sense it is all narrative, not only the historical books and the synoptic Gospels, but also its songs, its psalms and its epistles ; and in this sense it requires one type of understanding, a merely narrative understanding. But the Bible is also the vehicle of God's Word to us by which He claims us for Himself, by which we ourselves are confronted by His grace and are brought into living fellowship with God ; and here it demands a different understanding. The Bible then, is the Word of God in two senses, in a narrative sense, for it is *about* God and His Word spoken to others, and in a clamant sense, for it becomes God's Word spoken *to* us. It is *both* the record of, and the witness to, God's Word spoken to men and women long since dead, *and* the vehicle of His present Word to those now living ; and that difference can be expressed as a difference between two understandings of the Bible, a merely narrative understanding of its language and one that is clamant and literally urgent. Yet, while it is true that the difference is one between these two understandings, it would be error to suppose that it is merely that, for these two understandings themselves correspond to two different uses, a merely narrative and informative use and one that is addressive and clamant. It is only by the action of God Himself, by the use He makes of His own word, by the work of His Spirit, that the Bible can become God's Word to us who read and hear it. It is not a matter of sheer accident that we bring to His Word the one type of understanding or the other, nor is it a matter of our free untrammelled choice. If He did not speak to us we could not hear. It is not the manner of our understanding but His free Spirit that witnesseth with our spirits that we are the children of God. Yet if He speaks to us by His Word, as He is pleased to do, we are wilfully deaf who do not hear, wilfully and sinfully deaf, and fully responsible for our sin. The difference, then, between God's Word as witness and record and God's Word as vehicle and instrument is not *merely* a matter of two different understandings—to say that would be to take for granted His grace which is the last thing any man should take for granted. Yet there is a difference between two understandings involved, and, as we have seen, the difference is not that between a total mis-understanding and a true understanding, nor yet that between a dispassionate understanding and (shall we say ?) an existential one, but between a merely narrative understanding and a clamant one, between an understanding that such and such is the case and a similar understanding in which, nevertheless, a personal claim and claimant are present and are acknowledged.

It must be allowed, however, that this new understanding does reveal misunderstanding in the old ; and on this aspect of the matter David's reaction to Nathan's parable is again instructive. It is significant that his indignation was righteous indignation, and that in the dispute between the poor man and the rich, David was unreservedly on the side of the former. Similarly the natural man in his narrative and natural understanding of God's Word, as it unfolds the story of God's controversy with His people, unhesitatingly places himself on God's side of the fence. In the same way did the Pharisee, praying with a publican in the temple, place himself, with no thought that this might be a complete distortion of the facts. It is only the new understanding, when God's present voice is heard, that reveals a very different situation and leads to a re-interpretation of the old. For in the light of the new we are universally convicted of sin, of being not only over against God but also against Him, of having turned the narrative of His created world, from the most distant star to our daily bread, the narrative of His law written in our hearts and consciences, and even the narrative of His Word of grace and mercy and atonement, of having turned the narrative of *all* God's dealings with us into *mere* narrative, and of having turned His world into ours. We see that in the light of this revelation, sin cannot be defined or adequately described in relation to what is only a part of ourselves ; it is an alienation of the whole man from God, in his reason as well as his will, in his understanding no less than in his conduct of life. Moreover, so far as reason is concerned, it is not simply a matter of putting error in place of the truth, but of taking half-truths for the whole, mixing understanding with misunderstanding, and reducing to narrative and information the clamant language of life in which deep calls unto deep, so that seeing we see but do not perceive, and hearing we hear but do not understand. In similar fashion, as far as will is concerned, God, as living Person and sovereign Will, is driven out and man takes His place, so that God's law is reduced, even in its imperative form, to a mere narrative, to a human and humanly manageable code ; and even the Word of God's grace may be drawn into the circle of man's life as no more than a satellite in a man-centred universe. By God's living Word, spoken and addressed to us, we are convicted of sin in being redeemed from it and claimed for God and God alone ; and it is because He speaks, it is because He is pleased to speak, that we can hear and respond. But in hearing we know that He has spoken all along, in the things that gave us birth, in home and kin and country, in law, civilisation and conscience, in the Word made flesh and in the record thereof. If God spared not His own Son but delivered Him up for us all, how shall He not also with Him freely give us all things ? If God spared not His own Son but delivered Him up for us all, how shall He not also give Himself to all men and at all times ?

I have sometimes felt [said David Smith Cairns][1] that when we see the Lord, there will be something very familiar about Him, something that will remind us of all our youth, of all our dearest friends and kindred, because He was in them all, reaching after us in every dear one.

I cannot remember a time [says Principal John Baillie][2] when I did not already know that what my parents demanded of me and what they knew to be demanded of themselves were in the last resort one and the same demand, however different might be its detailed application to our different situations. I cannot remember a time when I did not know that my parents and their household were part of a wider community which was under the same single authority.

---

[1] D. S. Cairns, *An Autobiography* (S.C.M. Press, 1950), p. 33.
[2] *Our Knowledge of God*, pp. 182f.

Dr. Barth is perfectly right when he insists that if God did not speak we could not hear, that revelation is an event ; but he is wrong if he suggests or implies that if revelation is an event it is relatively rare and apparently arbitrary in its occurrence. God who speaks in Christ is One who will not keep silence. It is not that God's hand is shortened that He cannot save, nor His ear heavy that He cannot hear, nor His saving concern less that He will not speak. It is always our sin, and that only, which separates us from God. Revelation is an event ; it is not a factor in our environment of which we may take account when we please ; it is an event which is always happening everywhere and in relation to which there are only two possibilities open to us, sin and salvation. In the light, then, of God's Word which He speaks to us we see that our earlier narrative understanding was also misunderstanding, and, more than that, that our misunderstanding was sin.

At this point our argument impinges upon a well-known controversy between Dr. Barth and Dr. Brunner. In the light of the revelation in Christ, in whom God addresses Himself to us, we have been unable to set any limit to the area in which God is present to His creatures. Rather we have been compelled to recognise His presence and His claim everywhere in human experience. Thus we affirm a revelation of God in nature and morality as well as in Christ, what is called a general, as well as a special, revelation. It is on this question whether or not there is a general revelation, that Dr. Barth and Dr. Brunner have taken opposite positions, the former denying and the latter affirming the existence of such a revelation. Neither seems to gain a clean-cut victory in the controversy and prove his case. On the one hand, Dr. Brunner seems entirely right when he resists Dr. Barth's contention that natural man is utterly ignorant of God and has in his life and experience no point of contact whatsoever for the saving revelation of God in Christ, which when it comes must be understood as literally, absolutely and in every way creating its own response out of nothing. Against such a version of the matter Dr. Brunner maintains that formally, though only formally, the *imago dei* in natural man remains intact as a point of contact for the revelation in Christ ; that corresponding to this formal *imago* there is a general revelation of God which has, however, no saving value whatsoever, which " is not sufficient in order to know God in such a way that this knowledge brings salvation," [1] and that materially, if not formally, natural man is a totally corrupt being. But in reply to this Dr. Barth convincingly demands,[2]

How can Brunner maintain that a real knowledge of the true God, however imperfect it may be (and what knowledge of God is not imperfect ?), does not bring salvation ? And if we really do know the true God from his creation without Christ and without the Holy Spirit—if this is so, how can it be said that the *imago* is materially " entirely lost ", that in matters of the proclamation of the Church Scripture is the only norm, and that man can do nothing towards his salvation ? Shall we not have to ascribe to him the ability to prepare himself for the knowledge of God in Christ at least negatively ?

The difficulty is plain. On the one hand, we see, Dr. Brunner holds to a grace which is impotent to save, a merely preserving or sustaining grace, and on the other Dr. Barth clings to a gracelessness which is beyond comprehension and belief. The dilemma they present is not easy to resolve. Nor, let it be noted, is the solution brought any nearer by Dr. Barth's later recognition that there is in natural man an image of God which sin is impotent to destroy, for Dr. Barth continues to deny a general revelation as vigorously as ever, and, when the image is posited in the form of a fair and factual measure of mutual helpfulness, nothing has been said to alter a gracelessness no less incredible than before. Yet, if the image is described in a way which suggests the full faith

[1] " Nature and Grace," *Natural Theology*, p. 26.
[2] " No ! ", *Natural Theology*, p. 82.

and obedience of a Christian man, it has now been replaced by a gracefulness equally incredible when attributed—as Dr. Barth falls under the suspicion of attributing it—to man in general. Moreover, even if Dr. Brunner were to allow that the general revelation has some saving value, the clear conviction of universal sin would then be called in question, and the necessity for us of the revelation in Christ would become a matter of degree. There is no real and final escape from the dilemma with which the teachings of Dr. Barth and Dr. Brunner confront us by bringing obscurity, confusion and ambiguity into the doctrine of universal sin, and by bringing some, perhaps hidden, qualification to the properly clear conviction that Christ comes to us all as wholly and completely Saviour. The fact seems to be that Dr. Brunner's position lies nearer to the truth than Dr. Barth's. But it is involved in error and contradiction, mainly by reason of the very rigid divisions in terms of which it works—the rigid division on man's side between a pure, but purely formal, *imago dei* and its totally corrupt content, and the rigid division on God's side between a general but merely preserving grace and the special, the only saving, grace present in Jesus Christ.

What then is the truth? It is that God is present to us at every point of human life and experience, present in the created world around us and in the claim of morality upon us, above all present in Christ His Son. But there are two sides to this fact, and Dr. Brunner is quite right when he says that " we have to make the significant distinction between the subjective and the objective factor." [1] Clearly, there is on the one side what God does, and there is on the other what man makes of it. Dr. Brunner is also right when he goes on to say that " we may correctly characterise the objective and subjective factors thus : man misrepresents the revelation of God in creation and turns it into idols " ; [2] but unfortunately this insight has to be fitted into the

[1] " Nature and Grace," *Natural Theology*, p. 26. [2] *Ibid.*, p. 26.

rigid divisions both on man's side and on God's, to
which, as we have already seen, Dr. Brunner has committed himself.   On the other hand, if we put these
divisions aside and seek to understand the situation in
terms of the distinction between a narrative and a
clamant understanding, we find that the difficulties
which beset us may be avoided.   God is present to us in
creation and morality as well as in Christ, and the language of creation and morality is accordingly a clamant
language ; but apart from Christ our understanding of
it is a merely narrative understanding, in which God
becomes at the most a mere object of our thought of
whom account may be taken.   In this narrative understanding of the created world around us we may deny
God " with the top of our minds ", as Dr. John Baillie
puts it, or we may affirm His reality and may even prove
His existence after the manner of natural theology and
its theistic proofs.   Whichever course we take, we are
never in total error.   What we say may indeed be
largely true, even if, as in the case of the theistic proofs,
it is a rationalisation of what we already believe.   It
need not be the result of merely dispassionate, detached
and spectatorial thought ; but it is a merely narrative
understanding of the situation, and although it is not
altogether false it is thoroughly sinful, for we are there
self-possessed at the centre and God is on the fringe, on
the circumference of what is fundamentally *our* existence.
The salient fact in our experience of the created universe
is that we are a part and yet not a part, at home in it and
yet somehow pilgrims and strangers who seek a more
permanent habitation, so that this one is at most a
temporary lodging.   However we think of this situation,
apart from Christ, our understanding of it is merely
narrative, not wholly mistaken, but, in the light of the
revelation in Christ, entirely sinful.   The God who
speaks to us through the medium of His creation is
reduced to One about whom we do all or most of the
speaking.   No doubt even on this level and within this

area there are isolated experiences which overflow the merely narrative understanding of them, but they do not provide the means for a better understanding. When we seek to interpret and understand them and to adjust ourselves to them, we inevitably force them into the mould of our own self-contained thought. Our lives are continually invaded by the Divine, but the Invader is assimilated to and absorbed into the fundamentally and essentially *human* world which our sin has made, a world in which the clamant is reduced and subordinated to mere narrative. Moreover, this is so, not by a defect of grace, but as an effect of sin.

It is well, however, to remember that it is only by a distorting abstraction that we can separate the revelation in creation from that in morality ; and, short of Christ Himself, it is in the latter that God speaks most clearly to us. Indeed, it may well be questioned whether we could be aware even of other human beings if we did not stand to them in the mutual relationship of moral obligation. But here too, and perhaps above all, a similar account must be given. In our consciousness of moral obligation and in our moral life we are involved neither in total error nor in complete moral corruption. Some of us are better than others in certain respects, but all are mixtures of good and bad. Yet our understanding of this clamant situation is a merely narrative understanding, in which even the law of God is reduced to the scale of a manageable code, upholding a system of human life in which man is at the centre and God, if He is acknowledged to be there at all, is at the fringe. In a passage in which he has already paid tribute to Kant's rediscovery of the Primacy of the Practical Reason, Principal John Baillie has this to say of Kant's finished account of ethics.

The reduction of the spiritual life of mankind to the mere respectful acceptance of a formula was, in fact, the last absurdity of the eighteenth century. It is no mere formula with which the sons of men have ever found themselves faced as they approached life's most solemn issues, but a Reality of an altogether more intimate and personal kind.[1]

This is a perfectly just verdict upon Kant's moral theory when it is judged from the standpoint of ultimate truth, from the standpoint of Christian faith. The absurdity of Kantian ethics is not an intellectual absurdity to be seen and detected by the light of natural reason alone, it is a spiritual absurdity apparent only in the light of the revelation in Christ. Even the twentieth-century intuitionists who seek to do greater justice to the personal claim involved in morality find themselves compelled, when they try to understand the system of such claims, to look for the criterion of duty in something as impersonal as the tendency of an act to be right, the tendency of what they call a *prima facie* duty to be a duty. Elsewhere than in God there is no place where the truly personal source of morality may reside, and God as really God only comes to natural men in Christ, in coming to them there as man. He comes as God in morality and creation but is regarded as man, as human, as the indirect conclusion of a theistic inference or as the distant author of the moral law. Only when He comes as man in Christ is He received as God indeed. The understanding of morality apart from Christ is not completely mistaken, whether it follows the ethics of Kant or some other moralist, and natural men are not totally depraved ; but this understanding is a merely narrative understanding, and as such it is spiritually absurd and entirely sinful. Whether in thought or in life, sin *is* absurd in the light of Christian faith ; and as we have said the narrative understanding comes as an effect of sin and not by a defect of grace.

It ought to be noticed that this interpretation of the situation, in terms of the distinction between a merely narrative and a clamant understanding, clearly avoids, not only the doctrine of total corruption, but also the artificial modification of this doctrine by means of a

[1] *Our Knowledge of God*, p. 158.

rigid division between a perfectly pure form of the *imago dei* and an utterly corrupt content. Indeed this interpretation of the matter discards the conception of the *imago dei* itself in so far as that conception involves an attempt to understand and describe human nature apart from its present relationship to God. "The truth is," as Dr. John Baillie has finely expressed it,[1] "that there is in man no *nature* apart from *revelation*. Human nature is constituted by the self-disclosure to this poor dust of the Spirit of the living God." So far, then, this interpretation does seem to avoid some of the difficulties in which Dr. Brunner's position is involved in its attempt to bring Barthianism into closer accord with the facts. But the question arises whether it also suggests a more adequate account of grace than that which rigidly separates a wholly non-salutary, a *merely* preserving, grace from the only saving grace present in Jesus Christ ; whether, therefore, it suggests an account of grace which would avoid the critical questions which Dr. Barth has addressed to the other.

In this connection two points require to be noticed. In the first place, it must be remembered that God's ultimate purpose is not to be characterised without qualification as a purpose of salvation. It is a purpose of salvation only in relation to the fact of sin ; and, although we men, being sinners, may not be able to understand it apart from that fact, that is to say, except as wholly a purpose of salvation, we must be on our guard against arguing and thinking as if we could understand God's purpose as it would be in a world entirely devoid of sin—we have no right to assume that all revelation, if it is really revelation, must therefore be *saving* revelation. In the second place, there seems no reason whatever for holding to a rigid separation of general and special revelation, of general and special grace—so rigid a separation that the former must be conceived as merely preserving, whereas the latter alone

[1] *Ibid.*, p. 41.

is salutary. Is it not the one God who is revealed in both, and is not the revelation in Christ the fulfilment of the other ? And, therefore, is not the general revelation a saving one in the sense that it leads men to Christ, prepares them for Him in whose name only there is salvation ? It would fail in this preparatory work, it would be doomed to failure, only if it were totally misunderstood by men, but that we have seen not to be the case. God sustains us and preserves us by His grace, but in so doing He prepares us for the coming of His Son who is the final fulfilment of the divine revelation. Because our narrative understanding is not total misunderstanding, we are, indeed, prepared for this coming. But when Christ comes He comes as Judge as well as Saviour, for our narrative understanding *is* also misunderstanding, at the very point where misunderstanding is sin, at the very point where the clamant becomes merely narrative and what is fundamentally God's world is transformed into one which is fundamentally man's. Thus the proper distinction is not between a merely preserving grace and a saving grace but between one which preserves and prepares and one which saves. Only the theological recognition of this truth leaves room for the twin facts, first, that as we are faithful to the light which we have, often more light is given, and, secondly, that in betraying the portion of light that is ours we always betray a much greater light than we know.

The distinction, then, between a merely narrative and a clamant understanding seems to maintain itself amidst the difficulties with which the controversy between Dr. Barth and Dr. Brunner was largely concerned ; and, corresponding to this distinction, there are two different senses in which the Bible is the Word of God, for it may be the witness to, and report of, God's Word spoken to others, and it may also be the vehicle of God's Word spoken to us. A question, therefore, now arises regarding what happens when the Word of God comes home to us, when its clamant language is heard and acknowledged. What happens then is not that a number of propositions, a set of beliefs and doctrines, is imparted and imposed. Rather, a situation is created in which man finds himself confronted by God, sinful man face to face with a redeeming God. Here he discovers, not that he believes in God (he may have believed before, in a sense) but that God believes in him, that he is not his own but is bought at a price. This is a situation in which God claims the man for Himself (" I have called thee by thy name, thou art mine "), in short, the characteristic Biblical situation.

In the creation of this situation God may use the Bible, the record of His Word spoken to others ; He may use the preaching and proclamation of the Church which is based upon the Bible, or its creeds and confessions which are similarly founded : indeed, we cannot set a limit to what God may use in the fulfilment of His saving purpose. Moreover, when He uses the Bible, the Church's preaching or its creeds and confessions, the narrative understanding of these is not left behind ; but it is no longer a *merely* narrative understanding, it is caught up into a spiritual context, a personal situation, a living fellowship, in which deep calleth unto deep and the Spirit of God witnesseth with our spirits that we are the children of God. The narrative understanding is the medium through which God speaks. The fact that this narrative understanding does become a medium of God's present Word may well be an indication that this narrative understanding is not a total misunderstanding and misrepresentation, an indication, perhaps, that so far as it goes it is substantially true. But it does not follow in the least that this narrative understanding is either a complete understanding or an understanding perfect so far as it goes, that it is thereby guaranteed against both ignorance and error. On the contrary, we may be sure that ignorance is always there, that we always go out, in faith, like Abraham, not knowing whither we go. The history of religious thought makes

it clear that intellectual error, even intellectual error
with regard to God, revelation and faith, is by no means
the most grievous obstacle to a living fellowship with
God ; for men have communed with God across the
breathless air of rationalism, just as radical empiricists
at the present time enjoy the society of their fellows and
write books for their edification while being driven irre-
sistibly in their philosophy towards solipsism.   Thus, it
is clear, not only does the Word of God primarily create
a situation rather than impart and impose a set of beliefs
and doctrines, but, even in a secondary fashion, it offers
no guarantee of inerrancy nor does it provide a fixed
and final theology.   To suppose that it does is to take
the medium for the greater Reality that it mediates.   It
is only God who is the same yesterday, today and for
ever, not our thought about God, not even our thought
in acknowledged obedience to His revelation of Himself
in Jesus Christ His Son.   The revelation of God in Christ
certainly creates a situation and, moreover, a situation
in which faith is born as the gift of God ; but even in this
faith there may be some intellectual error, some element
of misapprehension.   There may be more, perhaps, in
the theological thinking which results when faith reflects
critically upon itself and the relationship to God in which
it stands.   We are, therefore, never free from the duty
to clarify our faith and to purge our theology and our
philosophy of life in general of inconsistency and error ;
and in the fulfilment of this obligation we are not by any
means committed to the perilous venture of working out
" an independent theory, gnosis or speculation."   For
the essential mark of such a venture is not the appearance of clear and consistent thinking in place of thought
which is inconsistent and obscure (on the contrary, as
John Oman said,[1] " obscurantism is already unbelief "),
but the substitution of a merely narrative understanding
for one that is clamant.   This task of progressive clarifi-

[1] J. Oman, *Vision and Authority* (Hodder and Stoughton, 2nd edition,
1928), p. 23.

cation is an endless one in which the mind of man is called to work in obedience to the revelation of God in Jesus Christ. In its performance there is no guarantee against error, but that does not render it a matter of idle speculation. It is indissolubly linked with the life of the Church, for its aim is to purify and clarify the human medium through which the living Word of God may be heard ; and, although intellectual error is certainly not the most grievous obstacle to a living fellowship with God, it may, none the less, be an obstacle to the propagation of the Christian Gospel.

Moreover, the recognition that the narrative understanding is not left behind when the clamant language of religion is heard and acknowledged enables the theologian to do justice to an aspect of Christian faith for which Dr. Barth, for example, can find no room. In a remarkably sympathetic appreciation of Barthianism H. R. Mackintosh took exception to what he called Dr. Barth's " excessive actualism ", " his persistent tendency to stress what may be called the dynamic aspects of Christian faith and life at the expense of the static." Mackintosh was thinking of the fact that to Dr. Barth " the whole idea of a ' state ' appears to be distasteful." " His aversion to the idea of a *state* of personal Christianity is unconquerable. Faith and regeneration are not conditions into which grace brings men, but bestowals from moment to moment." [1] This aspect of Dr. Barth's theology is intimately bound up with his conception of revelation as a sheer event, and, although there is important truth behind these characteristic contentions, Dr. Barth barely disguises from himself the disrupted version of the Christian life as a number of isolated events which they entail whenever they are made absolute. Dr. Barth's difficulties arise from the fact that he has presented himself with an over-simplified dilemma: either revelation is sheerly an event or else the Christian's knowledge of God is an independent gnosis indistinguishable,

[1] *Types of Modern Theology*, pp. 314, 315.

save perhaps in its conclusions, from the ordinary work of philosophy. If, indeed, these were the only alternatives it might well be necessary to say that Dr. Barth was right in the course he chose ; but, as it stands, the dilemma is by no means exhaustive, and the concept of the Christian life as a number of isolated but divine events is inadequate to the reality it seeks to describe. For although the believer's life is hid with Christ in God, although he lives by the Word which God, and God alone, can speak, there is continuity in his Christian life ; there is such a thing as a Christian state of existence, which becomes an illusion only when it, in turn, is made absolute. The means for understanding this more complex situation is to hand in the distinction between a narrative understanding and a clamant, and in the recognition that the former is not left behind by the latter. The narrative understanding, as it were, which is caught up into a living fellowship when its clamant character breaks through, and which yet survives, though perhaps not unscathed, the quickening encounter between the Spirit of God and the soul of man, provides the element of continuity in the life of the Christian, and is only discarded by the theologian who mistakenly insists that it must be either everything or nothing at all.

What, then, the living Word of God accomplishes is not in any way the transmission of an inerrant set of religious beliefs, but the creation of a religious situation, the Biblical situation in which sinful man finds himself confronted by the redeeming God. This is not to be confused with the situation of mere morality. The moral situation is, as I have argued elsewhere,[1] essentially a social situation, and as such it may well be a portion broken off and divorced from the Biblical situation, or rather from the original religious situation which the Word of God seeks to restore. Being such a portion, it may also involve a radical distortion within itself, so that the superstructure has become the found-

[1] Cf. *The Claim of Morality* (Gollancz, 1952), pp. 247-53.

ation, the implication has become the premise ; but that does not mean that it has ceased to be a real situation, that it is completely fictitious, with no grip whatsoever upon reality, and totally deficient both in truth and in goodness. Far from it. What the merely moral man sees may be true so far as it goes, and what he does not wholly bad. Otherwise, one can only suppose, the task of God's redeeming grace would not be a task of grace at all but, quite literally and absolutely, the task of a new creation, whereas, when God speaks in Christ, the language which He uses is not altogether foreign to those to whom He speaks. On the other hand, when He does speak, as He does in Christ, He creates a new situation which is not just an extension, a mere enlargement, of the old, but is the Biblical situation, a situation as old as the hills and yet for ever new, that total situation of which the merely moral situation is a broken fragment. In other words, when God comes into our moral social situation, as He does in Christ His Son, He does not come as one man amongst many, not even as *primus inter pares*, but as the least who is yet the greatest of all, as man who is no less than God and who as God is God indeed. This means that in being caught up into the new situation which yet is older than itself, the moral situation is subtly, but surely and no less thoroughly, transformed, and all the truth and goodness of which it was capable are reaffirmed while being re-oriented and fulfilled. It means that not just service, not just a series of obligations, but unending worship and gratitude are due to God ; it means that even our duties to others have their ultimate source neither in them nor in ourselves but in God ; and it means that what we owe to them is something far beyond the capacity of a merely manageable code to compute. " I say not unto thee," said Jesus, " Until seven times ; but, Until seventy times seven." The bond of this new situation is love, for we love Him because He first loved us, and its obligation is also love. " Thou shalt love the Lord thy God with all thy heart, and with all thy soul, and with all thy mind . . . and . . . Thou shalt love thy neighbour as thyself."

This situation, which we have described as the Biblical situation, is created by the living Word of God, by the revelation of God in Christ, arousing in man the clamant understanding which is involved in faith. It is distinguishable in principle from the moral situation, not only as it is ordinarily understood, but also as it might ideally be conceived; and it can be seen that this Biblical situation could only exist as the creation of God's Spirit, and could not conceivably come into existence as the result of human effort in thought, word or deed, no matter how closely that effort might approach to the realisation of the merely moral ideal. It is evident, moreover, that, if it is created, it is also sustained by God's grace and revelation; that nothing else could sustain it, and that nothing less would be given by the God who has revealed Himself in Jesus Christ His Son. But, even here, it is sustained through the medium of a narrative understanding, which is always in danger of becoming a *merely* narrative understanding, to which even the fullness of divine mercy and grace would appear as a single item in a fundamentally human and man-centred world. The stern reality of the moral life is not entirely left behind in the life under grace.

Brethren [wrote St. Paul], I would not that ye should be ignorant, how that all our fathers were under the cloud, and all passed through the sea; and were all baptised unto Moses in the cloud and in the sea . . . but . . . many of them . . . were overthrown in the wilderness. . . . Wherefore let him that thinketh he standeth take heed lest he fall.

CHAPTER IX

MORALITY AND MYSTERY

R EVELATION creates a situation and restores a
broken relationship, broken from man's side and
not God's.   In this situation sinful man is confronted by a redeeming God, who speaks to man through
the medium of his narrative understanding of the universe and of his own place and destiny within it, to
which many factors in life and experience will have contributed.   He speaks, especially, through the medium
of man's narrative understanding of the Bible, an understanding which thereby becomes not merely narrative
but clamant as well.   It is evident that this natural
narrative understanding is radically modified by the fact
of revelation, by the fact that God speaks, but it is not
rendered infallible, fixed and final, and it would be
improper to speak of human reason as being completely
determined by God.   Anything that is *completely* determined from outside itself is deprived of all spontaneity,
and must be conceived as wholly passive and entirely
impressionable ; but man's rational and spiritual nature
is rarely, if ever, that, is less so in its higher reaches than
in its lower, and is least of all in religion.   What man
apprehends of God in His gracious revelation of Himself
is due to revelation and to that alone ; it could not come
within the ambit of human thought and life were it not
for revelation and the fact that God in His sovereign
freedom and mercy is pleased to reveal Himself to men;
but it is inevitably coloured by the mind of man, by the
outlook and understanding of the individual man, and
by the intellectual climate in which he lives.   To seek
for an understanding which would be entirely devoid
of this human element is to cry for the moon ; it is
to seek for an understanding which would not be an

understanding at all.   Moreover, it would be quite misguided to assume or suppose that this human element is
always mistaken.   On the contrary, it is never wholly
false, and there is no escape from the patient, persistent
task of purging out the error that is there.   Nor is this a
task to which Christian faith can be indifferent, and which
it can, with an easy mind, leave to others to perform.
Truth can never be indifferent to truth, and the revelation of God in Christ is true—at least it is genuine and
arouses beliefs which are true.   This does not mean, of
course, that Christian faith depends for its validity on
the truth of any one philosophy, be it existentialism,
radical empiricism or Thomism.   Not at all.   It only
means that, taking its stand upon the truth of God in
Christ by which it lives, it has an inalienable interest in
the promotion of true human thinking, especially where
such thinking comes close to its own domain, so that
Truth may speak the more clearly through truth to the
heart and soul of man, although Christian faith knows
also that God can speak through human error, using even
the wrath of man to redound to His own glory.   Intellectual error is not the most grievous obstacle to faith in
God and fellowship with Him, but it is an obstacle just
the same ; and Christian faith can never be complacent
in face of such a creed as logical positivism which reduces
all religious statements literally to nonsense and proves
itself a more radical opponent than straightforward
atheism or honest agnosticism.   Taking its stand upon
truth and reality, and, in particular, upon the ultimate
source of all truth and the living centre of all reality,
God as He has revealed Himself in Jesus Christ, Christian
faith must always seek a more adequate understanding
of itself, of the world in which it lives, and of the revelation of God by which it comes into existence and by
which alone it can continue to survive.

Dr. Barth, more perhaps than any other theologian,
has made a stand against the intrusion of human truth
into the domain of theology.   Certainly he is prepared to

acknowledge that in practice it is impossible to keep such truth outside, at a distance, but it is always for him a serious embarrassment when it enters.   As a theologian, he says in his *Credo*,[1] " I am not free of all philosophy, but at the same time I am not bound to a definite philosophy.   All things are lawful for me, but nothing shall take me captive."   " What I must know as theologian is that it is not my job to make a synthesis but to go upon a *way* which leads from the matter that commands to the form that serves." [2]   " Practically it is inadvisable for the theologian to bind himself for too long a period or too much in principle to *any* conceptions.   That is, it is inadvisable for him to anchor himself systematically to any technical terminology." [3]   But, of course, in serious and sincere thinking a man cannot change for the sake of change, and insincerity and instability afford no solution to Dr. Barth's problem.   It is still with him in his *Doctrine of the Word of God*.

> In practice it is not in our power to prevent this inroad of philosophy into dogmatics.   Neither is it in our power to give to critically reflective human thought in practice such a relation to the divine object or such a determination in terms of it.   But it is, of course, in our power to keep before us the need for such a relation and definition, and therefore to refuse any philosophy this right of irruption, to give the last word not to any immanent regulations of critically reflective thought, not to any longing on the part of man's need for thought, but solely to the needs of the Object here called in question.[4]

But if deliberate insincerity is no solution, no better one is to be found by cherishing a will-o'-the-wisp as an ideal, by coveting an understanding which would be no understanding at all.   The truth is that Dr. Barth's problem here is no problem whatsoever.   Reason and revelation are not alternative and rival norms, for the latter is on the side of the object while the former is on the side of

[1] *Op. cit.* (Hodder and Stoughton, 1936), p. 184.   [2] *Ibid.*, p. 184.
[3] *Ibid.*, p. 185.   [4] *Op. cit.*, p. 94.

the subject and provides the indispensable means for the exaltation of revelation and for loyalty to it. Reason is a rival to revelation only when it takes the form of an outmoded rationalism and sets itself up as the sole and sufficient source of certain truth. But if rationalism is dead, except in a conscious and deliberate attempt to return to the mental outlook of the Middle Ages,[1] there is no reason why it should find a place in the forefront of our thought ; and, in any case, there is no need to fly to the opposite extreme in order to avoid it.

What may conflict with revelation is reality, or rather reason's conception of reality, reason's possibly mistaken thought about reality. Revelation can communicate in spite of human error (as it did in the ages of rationalism when men were claimed by the grace of God for His fellowship, although, under the influence of the prevailing philosophy of the day, they regarded Him as the conclusion of a human inference). But neither the human mind nor Christian faith can rest content in such error. In Dr. Barth's own theology, if our analysis and argument are to be trusted, there are, in spite of his clearly defined intention, human elements which are at odds with the revelation in Christ, elements such as the concept of men as *mere* creatures and the strain of radical empiricism which regards revelation as sheerly given. In this latter aspect of his thought Dr. Barth is certainly in line with what is in certain countries the prevailing philosophy of the present time, the logical positivism or radical empiricism which has taken the modern mind by storm. More accurately, Barthianism belongs with logical positivism to the same anti-rational reaction. It has a place in the same flight from reason, the same reliance upon that which is sheerly given, although of course in other respects it is in violent antagonism to this radically empirical school of modern philosophy. In the Middle Ages the tenets of natural theology were not in blatant contradiction to the characteristic beliefs of

[1] For an example, *cf.* Hawkins, *The Essentials of Theism*, p. 14.

rationalism in general ; but Barthianism, in spite of its kinship to, cannot claim any such harmonious relationship with, logical positivism, since the latter theory regards experience as the sole foundation of all human knowledge and all experience as sense-experience, and insists that any statement which goes beyond such experience, as almost all the typical statements of Barthianism undoubtedly do, is literally nonsensical and devoid of all meaning. Even cousins have been known to quarrel, and, in the last resort, Christian theology and logical positivism are ill-assorted companions. On the one hand, the revelation of God in Christ cannot be brought easily and without violence under the concept of that which is sheerly given, the radically empirical, and it rebels against the corresponding reduction of its appropriate response in faith to a mere " complete determination " of man's reason from without. On the other hand, logical positivism, in spite of its protests and in spite of its admitted transcendence of the dichotomy of mind and matter, belongs to the ego-centric tradition which has misled modern thought since the day that Descartes arrived at his famous argument, *Cogito ergo sum*, a day that was, according to William Temple,[1] " perhaps the most disastrous moment in the history of Europe." The appearance given of transcending the ego-centric predicament is not real transcendence at all, for it destroys even the ego in reducing it to a mere history of sense-contents and is working, therefore, with an abstraction from an abstraction. Ludwig Wittgenstein as a radical empiricist was perfectly consistent and clear-sighted when he declared that " what solipsism *means* is quite correct, only it cannot be *said*, but it shows itself." [2]

[1] *Nature, Man and God*, p. 57 ; quoted by John Baillie, *Our Knowledge of God*, p. 153. But is Temple's verdict quite fair to Descartes ? Was he not making explicit what had previously been implicit, namely, ego-centricity, except in so far as earlier thought had been shielded by the inadequate doctrine of a universal reason ?

[2] L. Wittgenstein, *Tractatus Logico-Philosophicus* (Routledge and Kegan Paul, 1922), 5.62.

Moreover, within this ego-centric tradition, logical positivism belongs to the strain of empiricism which John Locke instituted when he laid it down that all human knowledge is based upon the simple ideas of sensation and reflection, of outer and inner sense as it were. George Berkeley and David Hume continued this strain while endeavouring to rid it of inconsistency by eliminating elements of human knowledge which could not be thus empirically supported. Logical positivism thus stands aside from the system of Immanuel Kant who sought to set this movement in reverse, not modifying the concept of human knowledge to bring it into line with the experience which was held to support it, but seeking a more adequate conception of experience so that human knowledge could more securely be based upon it. In so doing Kant was led to work out the entire critical philosophy, a modern synthesis of faith and experience, of faith and understanding, of faith and science, one might say, which bears comparison with the medieval synthesis of St. Thomas Aquinas, and to which we shall have to give some further consideration.

Before leaving logical positivism it is as well to notice that if it contains any impulse towards religion, such an impulse is intermittent, and in no way leads in the direction of Barthianism. The liking of the latter for radical empiricism is, therefore, a clear case of unreciprocated affection. Just as the main logical positivist account of morality is emotive, holding that moral judgments are neither true nor false but that they express an emotion either of approval or of disapproval, so religion, if it finds a place at all and is not simply dismissed with all metaphysics as nonsense, appears as mysticism. It is on such a note that Wittgenstein brings his *Tractatus Logico-Philosophicus* to a close. " God does not reveal himself *in* the world," he says.[1] There is, in other words, no place for religion within the world and whatever can be said—in Wittgenstein's terminology it is only within the

[1] *Op. cit.*, 6.432.

world that anything can be said—belongs to natural
science.[1]   Religion is concerned with the world *sub specie
aeterni* and contemplates it as a limited whole.[2]   What
is apprehended in this contemplation cannot be said,
cannot be stated in propositions which are either true or
false, and cannot even, like an emotion, be expressed in
a statement which is neither true nor false.   " The feeling of the world as a limited whole is the mystical feeling," [3] and " for an answer which cannot be expressed
the question too cannot be expressed." [4]   " Whereof
one cannot speak thereof one must be silent." [5]   Indeed, contrary to the usual empirical treatment of the
subject, Wittgenstein holds that even " ethics cannot be
expressed," that " ethics are transcendental," concerned,
that is to say, not with something *in* the world but with
the world as a whole, that " ethics and aesthetics are
one," [6] and, presumably, that religion, in turn, is identical with both.   Nor is this introduction of mysticism
and the ineffable an afterthought of Wittgenstein's system, a summary treatment of subjects which present a
difficulty to radically empirical thought ; on the contrary, they are the end, it appears, towards which he was
moving from the beginning, so that his radical empiricism is, as he puts it,[7] simply a ladder to be used and
thrown away when one has reached the top.   Normally,
it might be thought, one demands a foothold much more
secure before acting in such a foolhardy manner ; and
yet that is all that Wittgenstein has to offer.   He gives
morality and religion a place on the very edge, the
thinnest possible edge, of the scientific world, and yet
suggests that the edge is much more important than anything else.   Moreover, there is a deep-seated and consistent logic in this movement of Wittgenstein's thought,
for if a standpoint is taken up within the ego-centric
tradition and, in particular, within the severe empiricism

[1] *Cf. Tractatus Logico-Philosophicus*, 6.53.
[2] *Cf. ibid.*, 6.45.   [3] *Ibid.*, 6.45.   [4] *Ibid.*, 6.5.
[5] *Op. cit.*, 7.   [6] *Ibid.*, 6.421.   [7] *Cf. ibid.*, 6.54.

long associated with the name of David Hume, even morality, still more religion, finds itself in a most precarious position.   In the end, it seems, morality must either take refuge in the emotions of approval and disapproval, which are themselves neither right nor wrong, proper nor improper, true nor false, or else it must take flight to the ineffable, the whole of what is experienced, which cannot even be expressed, still less stated in propositions that are true or false.   Religion in turn is faced with an even more radical dilemma, for it must either disappear altogether, since there is no place for it within what is experienced, or else identify itself with " the feeling of the world as a limited whole," the mystical, the ineffable, that which cannot be expressed, in which all differences, and, incidentally, all difficulties, are miraculously eliminated.   Wittgenstein has seen this with admirable clarity.   In the Preface to his book he declares that " its whole meaning could be summed up somewhat as follows : what can be said at all can be said clearly ; and whereof one cannot speak thereof one must be silent." On the one side, there is science, without mystery and without depth, and on the other side there is mystery, so great that one cannot begin to express it, so profound that the moment one begins to speak of it one is inevitably using words without a meaning.[1]

Radical empiricism, however, is not the only strain in modern philosophical thought.   Broadly speaking, it may be said that modern philosophy has been taken up with two alternative and alternating tasks.   Sometimes it has endeavoured to restate human knowledge in varying ways, even dismissing, as completely meaningless, certain elements which had crept into it, in order that it might be genuinely supported by a given simple conception of experience ;   while at other times it has set itself the task of working out a more adequate idea of experi-

---

[1] In all this we are concerned with an important movement in Western thought, and it is not to our present purpose to take account of later developments in Wittgenstein's own thinking.

ence, upon which human knowledge could be more
securely founded.   Immanuel Kant is the great origin-
ator and exponent of the latter method of thinking
philosophically, and it stands to his great credit that he
produced the critical philosophy, a modern synthesis, we
have said, which will stand comparison with the medieval
synthesis of St. Thomas Aquinas.   Yet it is principally
valuable to contemporary thought as a synthesis of problems rather than as one of solutions, the problem of
experience and the knowledge it supports, consisting
mainly of science, the problem of the limits of this knowledge (with which even Wittgenstein was concerned in
his own way, for his aim, in other words, was " to draw a
limit . . . to the expression of thoughts "), the problem
of morality and other selves, and, in the most intimate
connection with this, the problem of religion and God.
Perhaps than that no better summary and synthesis
could be given of the questions and problems with which
religious and philosophical thinking is concerned at the
present time.

    In the hands of Kant, however, these problems did not
remain problems awaiting their solution.   Kant himself
had his own answers, and fundamentally he had two
major points he wished to make.   In the first place, he
argued that experience is much more complex than
Locke, Berkeley and Hume had assumed, since its com-
ponents were not entirely simple ideas sheerly given but
were also, some of them, contributed by mind, and since
mind in the form of understanding was active even in
experience.   This was only the first instalment of Kant's
answer to David Hume, but, although its validity can be
questioned—and has been questioned, for example, by
the radical empiricists, who prefer to go back beyond
Kant to Hume—it has at least revealed to the philosophical mind the possibility of seeking a more adequate
empiricism, an empiricism which would work with a
more adequate concept of experience.   This was no
small contribution that Kant made, for it may well turn

out that the task he thus depicted is the fundamental task of modern thinking.   If empiricism is the alternative to a rationalism which can no longer win confidence in itself, then there is, on the other hand, something radically wrong, something totally inadequate, in an empiricism which finds itself invariably on the verge of solipsism.

Important, however, as this side of Kant's critical philosophy undoubtedly is, both in its general intention and in its detailed execution, Kant's second instalment of his answer to Hume is even more important.   It consists of his far-reaching principle of the Primacy of the Practical Reason, for Kant holds that through our moral life and experience we have a deeper insight into the nature of ultimate reality than we can obtain through the medium of ordinary experience.   Yet this statement as it stands requires modification if it is to express precisely Kant's own position.   In the first place, we have referred to an insight into the nature of ultimate reality and that suggests a form of knowledge ; but Kant himself will not have it so, he deliberately rejects that possibility.   " I have found it necessary," he says in the Preface to his *Critique of Pure Reason*, " to deny *knowledge*, in order to make room for *faith*."   And yet Kant does not mean by faith something that cannot be expressed, like Wittgenstein's " feeling of the world as a limited whole."   Kant's faith is certainly not Wittgenstein's mystical feeling ; it is rather, and in comparison, a form of knowledge, but it is called faith because it cannot be convincingly and impartially proved, because it is simply postulated, though necessarily postulated, Kant believes, by moral or practical reason.   Kant is able to say what are the objects of this faith.   They are, he holds, God, freedom and immortality ; and it seems clear that it is only a narrow conception of knowledge which enables Kant to exclude faith and oppose the one to the other. In the second place, however, Kant would never speak of moral experience.   If faith is properly to be regarded as a kind of knowledge, it is not knowledge based on experience of any kind, it represents an inherent demand of our moral nature, of practical reason ; and if in recognising faith Kant has virtually recognised another kind of knowledge in some sense, he has not added a new empiricism alongside the other which he had already accepted ; he has instead placed an element of rationalism side by side with that other empiricism, but a curious form of rationalism, a moral rationalism which proceeds, not by rational argument about ultimate reality, but by means of rational demands upon ultimate reality.

Now there is great and valuable truth in Kant's contention. For one thing, it places the reality of God for us in indissoluble connection with our awareness of a claim that is laid upon us in morality. When we find God, we do so, not as mere spectators of a play, but as actors ourselves engaged in action, and if life and thought could ever fall utterly apart we can depend upon it that God would be on the side of life rather than thought. " If any man will do his will, he shall know of the doctrine, whether it be of God." God is not an object to be apprehended by mere thinking, by rational argument and speculative reason, a Being whose existence we can prove as we may demonstrate that the three angles of a triangle are together equal to two right angles. He does not first exist for us and then claim us as His own ; His reality is already from the beginning a more demanding claim than we yet know. Moreover, there is doubtless in the moral life, not only the recognition of a claim, but something akin to the making of a demand. In acting rightly we are, we perceive, at one with the stars in their courses, and reality itself, whatever it ultimately is, must approve, support and protect. It is not that we act rightly for the sake of protection and reward, for then we should not be acting rightly at all. It is rather that in recognising a certain act as *right* we recognise it as one which not only demands of us its performance but demands also of whatever gods there be its ultimate and complete vindication. What Kant does not see is that

moral or practical reason, in making its characteristic
demand upon ultimate reality in the form of God, freedom and immortality, is demanding something it already
possesses, and, although possessing It, demands It still,
because it insists on possessing this Other rather than
allowing this Other to possess it.

In spite of its merits, there are indeed two major criti-
cisms that must be levelled against this part of the Kantian system. In the first place, the religion which Kant
allows is of a most attenuated variety. God comes into
the picture as the mere rewarder of virtue, a mere appendix to morality, no less subject to the moral law because
He is never even tempted to depart from it. There is
nothing here of grace and forgiveness, of a God who
stoops to conquer, and there is nothing of His majesty,
the majesty of One who is Creator, Ruler and King,
whose is the law we ought to obey. The God of Kan-
tianism is both too remote and too near to satisfy the
Christian consciousness of God, too remote because manifestly He is not the God and Father of our Lord Jesus
Christ who dwelt among us full of grace and glory, and
too near because He differs from us in physical power
rather than moral standing, in stature rather than status.
But, in the second place, Kant's recognition of religious
reality is thus limited because it comes by the way of
rationalism. God is posited, not present ; and by that
very fact, in spite of his clear insistence that it is concerned, not with an inference of speculative reason, but
with a demand and postulate of practical reason, Kant's
theory classifies itself as a special case of rationalism.
Principal John Baillie has quoted Kant as saying that
" the purpose of prayer can only be to induce in us a
moral disposition. . . . To wish to converse with God
is absurd : we cannot talk to one we cannot intuit ; and
as we cannot intuit God, but can only believe in him,
we cannot converse with him." But, Principal Baillie
rightly remarks, " it is precisely such a sense of *converse*
with the Living God as Kant thus clearly saw to be

excluded by his own system that lies at the root of all our spiritual life." [1]

The truth is that Kant is firmly imprisoned in the ego-centric predicament no less than others, and perhaps the most impressive evidence of this fact is to be found in his principle of the autonomy of moral reason. The moral law comes not from without but from within ; it is a law which innate reason itself imposes upon man. If in morality we are claimed, it is by our own higher nature, by our practical reason, that we are claimed. Apart from the appendix of religion, the moral being is self-complete and self-contained, according to Kant. It is true that when he came to formulate the moral law, and, in particular, when he came to enunciate it as the law that one should act so as to treat humanity, whether in one's own person or in that of any other, in every case as an end withal, never as means only, he came within sight of the point at which he might have transcended his epistemological isolation. He even spoke of persons, that is, of rational beings, not rational laws, as an object of respect, and yet it is clear that they were so for Kant because being rational beings they produced such laws out of themselves, so that it might almost be said that for Kant persons in the full reality of their personality were mere occasions for showing respect for law ; and it is a serious gap in his system of thought that at this point he does not trouble to say how we know that there are other persons. The principle, he says,[2] " that humanity and generally every rational nature is *an end in itself* . . . is not borrowed from experience . . . because it is universal, applying as it does to all rational beings whatever, and experience is not capable of determining anything about them." But how then, it may well be asked, do we know that there are other moral beings ? If we do not know by experience, is it by rationalism that we are

[1] *Our Knowledge of God*, p. 159.
[2] T. K. Abbott's translation in *Kant's Theory of Ethics* (Longmans, Green, 1927), p. 49.

assured ?   Do we postulate them as we postulate God ?
Are they necessarily assumed occasions of right action
as God is the necessarily assumed rewarder of right
action ?   On such points, unfortunately, Kant is silent.
Had he raised this question he might have seen the limitations of his own thought at this point, and he might
have become aware that not his moral rationalism nor his
more adequate empiricism nor a synthesis and combination of the two was sufficient to transcend the ego-centric
predicament and produce a more satisfactory account of
the human situation.

Indeed it is precisely here, at the very point at which
Kant failed, that the contemporary schools of existentialism can claim a hearing, for in them, or in some of them,
the ego-centric predicament is decisively transcended
and the task of working out a more adequate empiricism
is enthusiastically embraced.   This is brought out clearly
by Gabriel Marcel in his Gifford Lectures on *The Mystery
of Being*, and especially in his chapter on " The Need for
Transcendence."   There he protests against two common errors, firstly, that of regarding the transcendent as
transcending experience, and, secondly, the prejudice
which, he says, dominated nineteenth-century thought,
that " all experience in the end comes down to a self's
experience of its own internal states." [1]   As against such
misunderstandings he insistently affirms that " there
must exist a possibility of having an experience *of* the
transcendent as such, and unless that possibility exists
the word can have no meaning." [2]   " The urgent inner
need for transcendence should never be interpreted as a
need to pass beyond all experience whatsoever ; for
beyond all experience, there is nothing ; "—so rationalism, moral or speculative, is decisively set aside—" I do
not say merely nothing that can be thought, but nothing
that can be felt.   It would be much more true to say
that what is our problem here is how to substitute a

[1] G. Marcel, *The Mystery of Being* (Harvill Press, 1950), Vol. I, p. 49.
[2] *Ibid.*, Vol. I, p. 46.

certain mode of experience for other modes." [1] " Consciousness is above all consciousness of something which is other than itself, what we call self-consciousness being on the contrary a derivative act whose essential nature is, indeed, rather uncertain." [2] Much later in his discussion he says that " if one thinks it over, one will also perceive that all human intercourse worthy of the name takes place in an atmosphere of real intimacy that cannot be compared to an exchange of signals between an emission post and a reception post," and that " in its own intrinsic structure " even " subjectivity is already, and in the most profound sense, genuinely inter-subjective." [3]

If it is the case that much modern thinking has been coloured and determined by an ego-centric assumption and prejudice it is clear that existentialism, in making such characteristic assertions, is highly relevant to contemporary philosophical discussion and deserves a very careful hearing. On the other hand, it must not be assumed that in steering clear of certain difficulties it does not run headlong into others. In his Encyclical Letter, *Humani Generis*, Pope Pius XII referred to the " new erroneous philosophy which, in opposition to idealism, immanentism and pragmatism, has assumed the name of existentialism, since it concerns itself only with the existence of individual things and neglects all consideration of their unchangeable essences," while, in the course of a much more detailed discussion [4] of the philosophical questions raised by the Encyclical, the Roman Catholic scholar Professor Albert Dondeyne has given a carefully argued and critical assessment of the new movement in which, although he reveals a sympathetic appreciation of many of its contentions, he finally judges that it leads in the end to the dilemma : either a denial of the divine transcendence or else an

[1] *Ibid.*, Vol. I, pp. 47f.   [2] *Ibid.*, Vol. I, p. 52.   [3] *Ibid.*, Vol. I, p. 182.
[4] A. Dondeyne, *Foi Chrétienne et Pensée Contemporaine* (Publications Universitaires de Louvain, 1951).

acceptance of mysticism as regulative of religion. And this verdict is not without some justification.

Existentialism certainly transcends the ego-centric predicament to which, as we have seen, so much modern thinking is tied, and it does this by means of its emphasis upon what it calls the intersubjectivity. On the other hand, it is equally concerned to overcome the abstract character of human thinking, in science for example, which is not interested in the particular as such but in the general, and so to grasp the concrete. Nor are these two aims entirely unrelated. When my neighbour personally confronts me, he does so invariably as an individual and not as a universal, and in so far as I think of him as an instance of a universal, as a member of a certain social class, perhaps, or as a supporter of a certain political party, so far I fail to be aware of him as an individual and a subject. On the other hand, when, as it were, we are thinking in general terms, when our concern is with natural laws and abstract conceptions, we are for the moment spectators of our own world, our situation is ego-centric, and we may or may not realise that as an ego-centric situation it is no more than an abstraction from our real situation, our real and ultimate condition of intersubjectivity. Thus these two aims of existentialist philosophy are not brought together in a completely arbitrary fashion ; but in existentialism they are so intimately and closely connected, they are so nearly assimilated, that the individual becomes an instance, albeit an especially important instance, of the particular, and the general condition of intersubjectivity is sometimes in danger of becoming little more than a check upon the extravagances and relativities of the individual's grasp of the concrete. Be that as it may, however, it is the case that, by virtue of its mutual assimilation of the two distinguishable tasks of doing justice to the condition of intersubjectivity and of laying hold of the concrete, existentialist thought is led to distrust conceptual thinking and to lay great stress upon action,

choice and feeling—not blind feeling, but feeling as participation in being, an openness to reality which is yet
essentially feeling and which is neither pure receptivity
nor pure activity. But here, I believe, existentialism has
taken the wrong turning and does run the risk of making
mystical feeling the norm of religion ; while in failing to
distinguish effectively the other subject who confronts
me from the concrete at large it is certainly in danger of
denying the divine transcendence—if it does not in fact
deny the divine reality, as it is led to do in one branch of
existentialism, that which is due to Sartre, Merleau-
Ponty and others.

It is, then, a curious fact that both on the side of
radical empiricism and on that of existentialism, two
widely and even extremely contrasting movements,
modern thinking tends towards a choice between atheism
(if that term may be used broadly for convenience to
cover even the reduction of all metaphysical statements
to the level of strict nonsense) and mysticism. But this
is the case. It is the case in radical empiricism because
this philosophy works itself out within the ego-centric
predicament ; and it is the case in existentialism because,
although it seeks to do justice to the condition of intersubjectivity, it does not succeed in fully transcending
the prejudice of ego-centricity. In one of his essays
M. Marcel maintains that " for Sartre, the awareness of
others is inseparable from the shock of the encounter with
what he describes as a ' freedom ', an alien freedom which
is adverse and threatening to himself,"[1] and he refers to
Sartre's " complete denial of *we* as subject, that is to say
. . . the denial of communion. For Sartre this word
has no meaning at any possible level." [2] While both
seek to achieve a more adequate approach to reality than
the severely spectatorial attitude of science, for example,
and positivism, the fundamental notion for Marcel is
participation, whereas for Sartre it is appropriation.[3]

[1] G. Marcel, *The Philosophy of Existence* (Harvill Press, 1948), pp. 51f.
[2] *Ibid.*, pp. 54f.   [3] *Cf. ibid.*, p. 55.

This is a most revealing comment, for it makes it clear,
first, that Sartre and Marcel, as representing what has
been called, respectively, closed and open, atheistic and
Christian existentialism, both re-affirm Kant's principle
of the Primacy of the Practical, not however as a form of
rationalism (that is, as a rational transcendence of experience), but within a higher or more adequate empiricism ;
and yet, secondly, that within this empiricism neither
lays the stress upon reason or understanding but upon
feeling, and the difference between them is a factual and
moral one comparable to that between Thomas Hobbes
and the Earl of Shaftesbury.   M. Sartre has simply substituted a moral and active ego-centricity for the spectatorial ego-centricity of the positivist, and it is by no
means evident that this is properly to be regarded as a
considerable gain.   M. Marcel, on the other hand, has
made a definite effort to transcend the ego-centric predicament, whether it be of the spectatorial or of the moral
and existentialist variety, but he has failed to do so since
for him also it is feeling which is fundamental.

M. Marcel certainly makes great play with the inter-
subjective condition which occupies an important place
in his thinking, but it is interesting and instructive to discover his precise conception of this condition.   In principle there are two quite different ideas he might have
entertained of it, one in which subject directly confronted subject, and the other in which two or more
subjects together, present to each other, directly confronted reality ;   and it seems to be the latter which
M. Marcel has chiefly in mind.   He has tried to transcend the ego-centric predicament of modern thought by
multiplying the number of egos, by placing them side by
side and uniting them by means of a bond of feeling ;
but in doing so he has failed to attain to the true moral
condition of intersubjectivity in which subject confronts
subject, in which subject claims and is claimed by subject.   " The more I free myself from the prison of ego-
centricism," he says, " the more do I exist," but by this

he means that " the more my existence takes on the character of *including* others, the narrower becomes the gap which separates it from being." [1] M. Marcel's theory of intersubjectivity makes frequent use of two ideas, that of presence and that of togetherness. Neither is unambiguous but Marcel's own intention is fairly clear. " Presence involves a reciprocity which is excluded from any relation of subject to object or of subject to subject-object." [2]

> When I say that a being is granted to me as a presence . . . this means that I am unable to treat him as if he were merely placed in front of me ; between him and me there arises a relationship which, in a sense, surpasses my awareness of him ; he is not only before me, he is also within me. [3]

Marcel can even say of an encounter that " it has developed me from within, it has acted in me as an inward principle " ; [4] and elsewhere he speaks of charm as one of the ways in which presence makes itself felt. Charm, he there tells us,

> is non-objective but it is intersubjective. However, even the term " intersubjectivity " might give rise to misunderstandings, for one might conceive of a content—still an objective content—that could be, as it were, transmitted from subject to subject. But the very notion of transmission must be excluded at this level of discourse ; the communion in which presences become manifest to each other, and the transmission of purely objective messages, do not belong to the same realm of being ; or rather . . . all transmission of objective messages takes place, if we may so put it, before we have yet reached the threshold of being. [5]

Marcel's idea of togetherness is employed in the same way. He lays great stress upon the preposition " with " in this connection. To be together is to co-exist, [6] and he speaks of a shared secret " as a mainspring of intersubjectivity." [7] If my neighbour is more than an object

---

[1] *The Mystery of Being*, Vol. II, pp. 34 and 33 (italics mine).
[2] *Philosophy of Existence*, p. 26.   [3] *Ibid.*, p. 24.
[4] *Ibid.*, p. 11.   [5] *The Mystery of Being*, Vol. I, p. 207.
[6] *Philosophy of Existence*, p. 25.   [7] *The Mystery of Being*, Vol. I, p. 178.

to me, if he is a subject and there is genuine intersubjectivity, then fundamentally I am not confronted *by* my neighbour, I am *with* him.   Fellowship is subordinated to fellow-doing and fellow-feeling, communion to a common task or interest, and not *vice versa*—and this not just intensively but extensively as well.   Here, however, Marcel puts the cart before the horse.   He tries to erect upon feeling [1] whatever moral order he can allow, instead of arousing, controlling and orienting feeling within an independent moral order, a genuine intersubjectivity in which deep calls unto deep and spirit encounters spirit.   It is not that Marcel has not given expression to important insights.   He has admittedly done so ; but he has fallen into error whenever he has been tempted to make these insights fundamental and has driven a wedge, has drawn an absolute distinction, between the realm of presence felt as the realm of being and every other realm such as that of an independent and objective moral order.   Without such an independent moral order it is a matter of arbitrary chance that Marcel's existentialism takes the course it does and not that followed by Sartre, while even along its own peculiar line the door is wide open to unbridled sentimentalism.   The other subject, for Marcel, is not one who confronts me and lays an objective moral claim upon me, but one who is present to me, a presence *felt*, as he affirms again and again ; and whether this ends in mysticism or sexual sentimentalism is, so far as one can see, a sheer accident.   In any case the ego-centric situation is not transcended if *my* feeling is the governing factor.   It is not transcended simply by setting a number of egos side by side, united by some bond of feeling, however deep.   It may be indeed that in this respect Sartre is nearer to the truth than Marcel, for he recognises the other self as a limit, although, it would seem, a limit to be resisted, not acknowledged.

It is evident from this discussion that the absence of an

[1] *Cf. The Mystery of Being*, Vol. I, pp. 199–201.

adequate theory of our knowledge of other selves is a major deficiency in contemporary philosophy. Outside the ranks of existentialism and its concept of the inter-subjective condition there seem to be two main schools of thought, neither of which can claim to have dealt adequately with its subject. On the one side, there is the inferential theory which holds that we infer the existence of other selves from what we observe of their bodily behaviour, while, on the other hand, there are those who identify our knowledge of other selves with our observation of their bodies and behaviour ; but both fail because both in their different ways offer us, not a knowledge of other selves made in the same image as we are, to whom we might address ourselves, but a knowledge of something to take the place of our knowledge of other selves, which is apparently and paradoxically assumed to be quite impossible. In short, the one school fails to provide an *awareness*, and the other to provide an awareness of *other selves* ; and yet no theory which denies the admitted fact of which it seeks to give an account can ever be deemed satisfactory. Indeed, so far as our awareness of other selves is concerned no theory can be considered acceptable which does not allow that in being aware of another person we are aware, at least, of a centre of thought and action, a point of view, a character, and a moral limit to our own existence. Other persons, it seems clear, are at least limits in that sense, in the acknowledgment of which there is none the less fulfilment. This was expressed by George Matheson in his hymn,

> Make me a captive, Lord,
> And then I shall be free. . . .
> My will is not my own
> Till Thou hast made it Thine ;
> If it would reach a monarch's throne
> It must its crown resign.

The existentialists have come very near to recognising this double truth of a moral limit which is also a fulfilment, perhaps even nearer than Kant, but they fail, it seems to me, precisely because they do not grasp the double character of the fact. For Sartre the other person offers a limit but no fulfilment, while for Marcel he offers fulfilment but no limit. In this connection Marcel's opposition between the notion of fulfilment and that of perfection is significant, for the former refers to " an experience of fulness, like that which is involved in love, when love . . . experiences itself as shared," and this belongs to " the order of the lived ", while the notion of perfection belongs to " that of the represented or conceived." [1] A moral order, too, would belong, presumably, to the realm of the conceived, but it is a mistake to drive a wedge between the concrete and the abstract, the particular and the general, the lived and the conceived. Thought is also life and life without thought is not life at the level of humanity. It is true that thought, even moral or practical thinking, may lose touch with life and become routine and formal, and contemporary existentialism may well be understood as a protest against the functionalised life of modern society, as Kierkegaard's existentialism was a protest against the conventionalised Christianity of the Church. But there is no salvation in mere life without thought, in life without principle. In the last analysis, while he may abuse Sartre and denounce his teaching as a " technique of vilification ", Marcel can have no rational complaint against him nor has he any rational answer to him within his own existentialist system. Such is life—without objective principle. There is indeed a difference between Sartre and Marcel, but it is a moral difference which can only be understood in terms of a moral order which cannot be derived from life alone but which belongs to life and thought together.

In saying this, however, I am simply saying what I have already said in other words, namely, that in entering the sphere of the clamant we do not leave that of the narrative behind. Life is not an alternative to thought but lights it up from within and is lit up in return. The

[1] *The Mystery of Being*, Vol. II, pp. 48 and 49.

moral judgment is not to be despised because, being a judgment, it belongs to the realm of conceptual thought. It belongs also to life and to the real. " Morality is the nature of things," as Bishop Butler said and P. T. Forsyth repeated. It is only in the moral order that the ego-centric predicament is genuinely transcended, and then only in a moral order conceived, not as a mere system of truth and still less as life without any grasp of truth whatever, but as a system of truth through which the clamour of life is heard. Marcel was wrong when he said that " the communion in which presences become manifest to each other, and the transmission of purely objective messages, do not belong to the same realm of being " and that " all transmission of objective messages takes place . . . before we have yet reached the threshold of being." On the contrary, it may well be doubted whether there is any such thing as the transmission of *purely* objective messages, and it seems necessary to affirm that every " encounter " is already to some extent a personal and moral encounter, however apparently formal and unlived it may feel. There are not two quite separate realms of being nor is there one of being and one of something else which falls below the threshold of being. There is one continuous realm or moral order, revealing wide variations in the matter of " presence felt ", verging at one extreme on the merely narrative, not the awareness of someone here but the belief that this is a person and that a person ought to be treated in certain ways, but even here never falling into complete error or total irrelevancy, never falling entirely out of connection with the upper ranges of the same realm. And in these upper ranges transmission, communication and narrative are not left behind. Communion does not exclude communication, the clamant does not exclude the narrative, but transfuses it ; and both the lower and the upper ranges, as well as the infinite gradations between them, belong to the one realm of being which is the moral order of reality.

To the modern mind, it is true, this moral order, when it is recognised at all, appears as an exclusively human order ; and yet in that conception of it there lurks a problem : Where is the centre, where is the ultimate seat and source of this order and its obligations ? For Kant that problem was disguised, since unwittingly he was still ensnared by the prejudice of ego-centricity, and where fundamentally there is only one rational will there is no real question about the seat and source of obligation ; but when that invalid assumption is firmly set aside the question becomes a live issue. It may be answered, and sometimes is, in offhand fashion by pronouncing in favour of the state ; but it seems little more than trifling to substitute the state for the moral in the dictum that the moral is the real. Within the bounds of natural or secular ethics the most that can be done is to point to the good, the *summum bonum*, the ideal system of personal relationships ; but in the final analysis that is not to solve the problem, it is only to postpone it. Moral philosophy may indeed place the ultimate source of obligation in the divine, but in doing so its affirmation is either formal or arbitrary. It is in the light of revelation alone that the centre of this moral order is really seen to be in God, in Christ ; but in Christ the centre is not only revealed, it is restored, and revelation deals with this situation in thought, this intellectual problem, only in the course of dealing with a far graver matter, a situation in life, the man-centred situation of natural humanity, in other words, with the universal fact of sin.

A distinction must be drawn here between two quite different predicaments, the ego-centric predicament of human thought and the man-centred predicament of human life. The former is a situation in thought which may darken and disturb our situation in life but which is invariably overflowed and belied by the latter. No man ever lives completely in a circle of solipsism. The man-centred predicament, on the other hand, is a predicament of life more than of thought, and, while it may

be contradicted by thought, it is not belied and transcended by thought alone. Solipsism is the denial of
other persons in thought and theory, but sin is the denial
of God in life and practice. It is with this latter condition that revelation deals by bringing God into the very
centre of our human world, God as man and all the more
really God because He has come so near, not only into
the world by His Son, but into *our* circumscribed world
by His Spirit. Here the ego-centric predicament and
the man-centred world are finally transcended, and sin
itself is overthrown. But it is man-centredness, not ego-
centricity, which is the essence of sin. Ego-centricity is
an aberration of thought more than of life. It is at most
a kind of blindness which obscures the revelation of God
in Christ and the fact of sin which it discloses and over-
comes ; but it tends to be *at least* that, so that men marvel
that they do not find God amid all the wonderful new
knowledge of an expanding science. But why, indeed,
should they think to find Him there ? On Easter morn-
ing He was not to be found in the lonely empty tomb,
but in the place where men might meet Him face to face
and other men as well. It was to the real world of men
and moral beings that He came, not to any mere abstraction from it, whether of theology, popular science or
positivism. The universe is not a spectacle to be observed but a stage on which men play their several parts
in the company of others—that is in effect Kant's principle of the Primacy of the Practical—and it is there that
God in mercy keeps tryst with men. Life is not a
scientific problem to be solved, but a challenge to be
met, a claim to be answered, and, in the last resort, a
claim upon us, not by men, but by God, a complete
claim upon all that we are and have. Nothing that we
know or think about the world of nature and the world
of men is quite irrelevant to this claim ; and yet when it
comes home to us, when its clamant language is heard
and understood, it not only corrects and completes both
thought and life, it brings a new abundance of life to both

in giving to each the same new centre, so that a man may well confess, " Whereas I was blind, now I see."

It is no *new* claim that is now made ; it is a forgotten commandment, an *old* claim which, by putting man at the centre in place of God, we have continually rejected. " Have I been so long time with you," said Jesus, " and yet hast thou not known me, Philip ? he that hath seen me hath seen the Father. . . . Believe me that I am in the Father, and the Father in me ; or else believe me for the very works' sake."

INDEX

ALTHAUS, P., 164

Answerability, moral, 48f., 50f., 129f.

Aquinas, St. Thomas, 3, 198, 201

Augustine, St., 3, 6, 15, 77f.

Ayer, A. J., 91

BAILLIE, J., 109, 113, 128n., 148n., 178, 182, 183f., 185, 197n., 204f.

Barth, Karl, 10ff., 15, 17, 18f., 22n., 25, 61f., 66, 68, 85–103, 104ff., 109, 110, 113ff., 123ff., 154–68, 169, 179–82, 185, 186, 189f., 194ff.

Barthianism, 10ff., 22f., 24f., 85ff., 123ff., 131ff., 154ff., 196f.

Bentham, J., 112

Berkeley, G., 198, 201

Brunner, E., 10ff., 61f., 68n., 72f., 76, 86, 104–8, 114ff., 120, 121, 122, 125f., 127f., 129ff., 169, 179–82, 185, 186

Buber, M., 50, 124

Butler, Joseph, 139, 141, 215

CAIRNS, D. S., 178

Campbell, C. A., 21, 34ff., 40f.

Carritt, E. F., 40

Character, 41f., 45f.

DESCARTES, R., 197

Dialectic, 137f., 168

Dondeyne, A., 207

EBNER, F., 124

Ego-centricity, 197ff., 205f., 208f., 215, 216f.

Empiricism, 6, 9, 198, 200ff., 206ff.

— radical, 90ff., 94f., 197ff.

— — in theology, 94f., 97ff., 124, 196f.

Existentialism, 124, 206ff.

FAITH, 11ff., 88f., 99, 150ff.

— as an event, 189f.

Farmer, H. H., 23n., 63

Forsyth, P. T., 10, 12, 15, 20, 80, 86, 87, 132, 134–43, 215

Freedom, 14, 17, 18, 40ff., 98f.

Fulton, W., 117

GOD, knowledge of, 148, 202ff.

Grace, 15f., 18, 62, 88f., 100–2, 127ff., 166, 180, 185f.

HAWKINS, D. J. B., 5n., 196n.

History, interpretation of, 116f., 132

Hobbes, T., 210

Holy Spirit, the, 76ff.

Hume, D., 198, 200, 201, 202

IKIN, A. GRAHAM, 36n.
Imago dei, 68n., 72f., 105f., 114, 119ff., 126f., 128, 137, 180f., 184f.
Intersubjectivity, 207, 209ff.
— as appropriation, 209ff.
— as existence in moral order, 183, 214f.
— as participation, 209ff.
Isaiah, 4, 20, 53f.

JOAD, C. E. M., 90, 91n., 124
John, St., 56, 58
Judgment, divine, 18, 19f., 21, 52ff.

KANT, I., 52, 167, 183f., 198, 201–6, 210, 213, 216, 217
Kierkegaard, S., 5, 124, 214

LEWIS, H. D., 21–34, 37, 40ff., 47n., 48, 89f., 94
Liberalism, 10, 86, 87, 88, 95ff., 130
Locke, J., 198, 201
Luther, M., 3f.

MACKINTOSH, H. R., 85, 92, 151, 153n., 154f., 164, 189
Macmurray, J., 6n.
Marcel, G., 206f., 209–12, 214, 215
Maritain, J., 3
Marx, Karl, 109, 110
Matheson, G., 213
Merleau-Ponty, M., 209
Mill, J. S., 8of.

Moberly, Sir Walter, 45, 47
Moral choice, 14f., 26, 34ff.
Morality, Christian, 18ff., 74ff., 8of.
— natural, 19f., 21ff., 31, 68ff., 72ff., 127, 139, 182f., 190f., 198, 200
Mysticism, 198ff., 207, 209

NEWMAN, J. H., 148
Niebuhr, Reinhold, 104, 108–22, 137

OMAN, J., 188
Other selves, knowledge of, 119, 183, 205f., 212f.

PATERSON, W. P., 10, 86
Paul, St., 3, 20, 34, 50, 52, 53f., 58, 72n., 80, 81, 93, 95, 96, 115, 192
Personal Christianity, state of, 189f.
Pius XII, Pope, 207
Plato, 6
Point of contact, 61f., 106, 114f., 117f., 137, 179f.
Pragmatism, 55
Pride, 26, 32ff., 53, 64

RATIONALISM, practical, 202
— speculative, 5ff., 135f., 149, 196
Responsibility, collective, 25, 26ff.
— legal, 26, 47, 48, 129
— moral, 14, 26, 34ff., 129f.

Revelation, 24f., 56f., 87, 88, 96f.
— general, 10, 105, 107, 179ff.
— special, 10f., 56f., 161, 164, 166, 179ff.
Ritschl, A., 5, 141f., 152–59, 164f., 167
Robinson, H. Wheeler, 79n.

Sartre, J.-P., 209f., 212, 214
Schleiermacher, F., 5, 149–54, 155, 157, 164
Shaftesbury, Earl of, 210
Sin, 21, 25, 26, 31ff., 34ff., 63ff., 125, 128f., 132, 137, 177f., 182ff., 216f.
Smith, Adam, 112
Smith, G. A., 76n.
Solipsism, 188, 197f., 216f.

Temple, W., 197
Theology, 12f., 55ff., 147ff.

Theology, evangelical, 10, 85ff., 123f., 130, 141ff.
— — ethical, 85, 104ff., 130f., 141ff., 168f.
Tillich, P., 7
Total depravity, theory of, 66, 67ff.

Understanding, clamant, 172ff., 182ff.
— narrative, 172ff., 182ff.

Wittgenstein, L., 197, 198ff., 201, 202
World, theological concept of, 31f., 63ff.

Young, A., 81

Zuurdeeg, W. F., 91